Cranberry Lake
from Wilderness to
Adirondack Park

Cranberry Lake
from Wilderness
to Adirondack Park

EDITED BY

ALBERT FOWLER

THE ADIRONDACK MUSEUM/SYRACUSE UNIVERSITY PRESS

To the Residents of Cranberry Lake
in Commemoration of
Their Centennial Year 1967

Preface

This book gives firsthand accounts of events in the Cranberry Lake region from 1845 to 1967. Arranged roughly in chronological order, the stories show the developing community through many eyes. There is little formal history, because in the main historians deal with their materials at second hand, sifting and arranging them in understandable wholes and patterns. These stories are the stuff of history before it comes into the hands of historians.

Cranberry Lake is part of the intricate network of lakes and ponds, connected by streams and canoe-carry trails, which stretches across the central and western plateau of the Adirondacks known as the Lake Region. It is the third largest body of water in the Adirondack Park, exceeded only by Lake George and the Sacandaga Reservoir. A century ago, it was nearly doubled in size by the completion of a dam, which backed water in long arms or flows up the valleys of feeder streams and flooded into extinction the cranberry bogs that had given the lake its name. Lying at an elevation of 1,486 feet, the lake is drained by the Oswegatchie River, which flows northwestward to the St. Lawrence at Ogdensburg. Encircling the lake are rounded hills and long ridges that rise from a few hundred to over a thousand feet above the surface. Gray cliffs and ledges accent the heavily wooded slopes. In the valleys between the hills are many small lakes, ponds, swamps, and beaver flows and meadows.

Although the stories collected here bear likeness to those told of other Adirondack lakes, there is one important difference. Because Cranberry was remote and hard to reach until the day of the motorcar, it was late in being developed. The earliest settlers came a generation or more later than did the first settlers on the Fulton Chain, on Raquette, Long, the Saranacs, and other large lakes of the Lake Region. Lumbering operations were even more retarded. In the Saranacs and along the Raquette River loggers arrived in the 1850's, simultaneously with sportsmen and tourists. But on Cranberry shores large-scale lumbering did not begin till the nineties. Sportsmen and summer residents had a long head start over lumbermen. They knew the lake as part of a wilderness little touched by civilization. Not till the 1920's had most of the primeval forest disappeared from nearby shores. Even today, Cranberry is wilder than any other large Adirondack lake. Forty of its fifty-five miles of shore line are part of the state-owned Forest Preserve. A few miles to the south lies a tract of fifty thousand acres that is probably the largest single stand of virgin timber left in the northeastern states. For purposes of study and research the Society of American Foresters recently designated three natural areas in this tract, each representing a different type of virgin growth.

Cranberry is the haunt of the woodsman born or made. The fashionable world has passed it by. Some of its seasonal residents and regular visitors have been well-to-do, and a few have been famous, but all have shared with people of the region a woodsman's love of the north woods and his adaptability. The stories of this book are by woodsmen and for woodsmen—even including the armchair variety.

I have had as colleagues in the preparation of this book Chandler Bragdon, retired history professor at the State University College at Plattsburgh, New York, Henry W. Bragdon, retired history master at Phillips Exeter Academy, Lois Dwight Cole, who has served as editor at William Morrow & Company and G. P. Putnam's Sons, and Hugh M. Flick, Associate Commissioner, University of the State of New York. Their long and intimate knowledge of Cranberry Lake and their wise counsel have helped shape the form and content of the following pages.

My colleagues join me in expressing appreciation for the valuable assistance that the following members of the staff of the Adirondack Museum gave in the preparation of this book: H. J. Swinney, director; Paul F. Jamieson, editorial consultant; and Warder H. Cadbury, research consultant.

ALBERT FOWLER

Rosemont, Pennsylvania
January 17, 1968

Contents

Illustrations

Illustrations (continued)

Maps

Cranberry Lake
from Wilderness to
Adirondack Park

CHAPTER I

Deer That Never Were Killed

"BOWLES"

IN 1852, when the following narrative appeared in the November 27 issue of *Spirit of the Times,* Cranberry was a little-known lake in primeval forest. There was no settlement on its shores or close by. The nearest cluster of houses was in the town of Fine, twelve airline miles to the west (twenty by the present state highway). From that hamlet "Bowles," author of the narrative, and his party proceeded over a crude road which ended at a landing on the Oswegatchie River ten miles below Cranberry Lake. No road reached the lake from any direction. The closest approach was made by two long-disused "old military roads," so-called because of the coincidence of their construction about the time of the War of 1812 and of their junction near Russell in St. Lawrence County, the site of an arsenal. One of these roads followed a northwesterly course through the Adirondack wilderness from the town of Chester in Warren County and passed through the Cranberry region several miles northeast of the lake. It became known as the Lake George Road after its extension at the eastern end. The other road has a long history. It began as an Indian trail (arrowheads have reportedly been found two and a half miles above Inlet Flow, where the old trail made its closest approach to Cranberry Lake) through the central and western Adirondacks from the Mohawk Valley to the St. Lawrence River. The first white man known to have journeyed through this region probably used this trail and reached the St. Lawrence River at the mouth of a tributary which, according to hints of its location, is almost certainly the Oswegatchie. He was a French Jesuit missionary, Father Joseph Poncet, who was released from captivity among the Iroquois in 1653 and escorted to the St. Lawrence. The story of his exhausting journey of ten days is told in volume 40 of Thwaites's edition of *The Jesuit Relations.* The same route may have been taken by Sir John Johnson and his Tory followers as they fled to refuge in Canada in 1776. The old trail started at Fish House, the sporting lodge of Sir William Johnson on the Sacandaga River, where it connected with a road to Albany. After improvement in the early nineteenth century, it became known as the Albany Road. But for want of traffic and upkeep, the wilderness sections of both the Albany and the Lake George roads soon reverted to hunter's trails, obstructed by saplings, brush, and windfall. Short sections were later cleared for lumbering operations.

Few records exist of the Cranberry Lake region before 1852. Between 1772 and 1800 several parties of surveyors, engaged in fixing the boundary between the Macomb and the Totten and Crossfield purchases, marked a line of trees through the woods five miles south of Cranberry Lake. After the American Revolution occasional white hunters and trappers penetrated the region. One of these, William Ward, is reported to have visited the lake about 1820. A state surveyor, Ebenezer Emmons, visited Cranberry during a rainstorm in 1839. When John Todd, Congregational minister, author, and pioneer tourist in the central Adirondacks, wanted a setting remote and hard of access for the beginning of his tale "The Doctor's Third Patient" (*Sartain's Magazine,* September, 1849), he chose the lake "called by hunters 'Cranberry Lake' and known only to them." The following narrative suggests that even hunters were infrequent visitors before 1852, for the party from Ogdensburg found an abundance of unwary game. A decade later, when Nathaniel Wheeler Coffin made a trip from Russell to Cranberry, the lake was still hard to reach. His party took a wagon over the Lake George Road for eleven miles southeast of Russell. Forced to abandon the vehicle, they continued on foot over the trace of the old road and then left it to head due south through trackless forest to the foot of the lake, crossing the Great Windfall on their way.

"Bowles" cannot be identified with certainty. Four articles on hunting expeditions in St. Lawrence County, all datelined "Ogdensburgh" and all apparently by the same author, appeared in the *Spirit of the Times* between February 3, 1849, and November 27, 1852. The first two and the last are signed "Bowles"; the third, "F. B. H." Miss Elizabeth Baxter, city historian of Ogdensburg, suggests that F. B. H. might be Franklin B. Hitchcock, coeditor and proprietor of the *St. Lawrence Republican,* an Ogdensburgh ("h" dropped in 1868) weekly. But dates present a difficulty. In July, 1848, Hitchcock sold his interest in the paper and went to California to hunt gold. Though he returned late in the year 1851 and bought back an interest in the *Republican,* he was in California at the time the first three of his hunting trips in St. Lawrence County allegedly took place. To identify Hitchcock as the author would require the assumption that the datelines are misleading, and that the first three articles at least describe events that took place prior to his departure for California in 1848.

You have passed sometime along the Mohawk and looked off northerly at the irregular mountainous horizon. In the bosom of those uplands lies Cranberry Lake. It is inaccessible to ease. Amateur sportsmen, who begrudge labor for a requital beyond the twi-r-r-l of a partridge, the whi-r-r-r of a woodcock, or the bark of a squirrel—all which may be had within the dong of a cowbell or the "how buck" of a hog gatherer—will never see Cranberry. Twenty-five miles through dense forest, over hills and up rapids, tax strength and constitution heavily. If either fail, there's no remedy—no pills, no powders, no emetics, no restoratives. Hence the solitudes of Cranberry are disturbed but seldom. The moose, the stag, find there congenial haunts, and the lake affords them a refuge against the fierce lolling wolf and panther.

At sundown, after leaving home, Old Mike—that name is legion—Otis, and Bowles stacked our surplus traps in the edge of the great forest, fifty miles from home. Our boat had suffered something by the heat and racking on the journey, but our stores and ammunition were all in prime order. We had terrible toil before us; so after supper we lay down early and slept soundly. Early next morning we had our boat lashed on an ox sled behind a pair of steers, whose owner had promised they would take it and our luggage easily seven miles through the woods to the foot of Stillwater, on the Oswegatchie.

Everything picked up and all ready, the driver swung his "jambock" [sjambok, a heavy whip]; "hush! haw!" but not a hush nor haw; only stooping heads and flying tails. "Woa-haw!" again he bawled, raised up his jambock, thrashed the cattle, blowed the cotton phlegm out the corners of his potato-hole, and yet no start. "Not so good a bargain at ten shillings, after all," thought I. "Yes, by ——, I thought so," said old Mike. Otis fired up. "That d——d off steer didn't pull a bit," and he twitched his rifle wiper out, sprang round the other side, threatened, gesticulated, yelled. Whang again went the jambock, and Otis flew at the steer: "Hie! h–ll! I'll knock your horn off!" and away they went around a turn, as I got a last glimpse of the stringy phlegm ("plug 'em") in the distended corners of that mouth.

Old Mike was vexed. I swore myself at Truax [a Daniel Truax was supervisor of the town of Fine in 1852], our guide and companion: "D——n him! he knew that steers can't go over this road; and he might have prevented, rather than encouraged, my ten shilling bargain." Soon we heard ahead the steers were stuck. Otis had gone back after his rifle, and neither howling, nor jambock, nor phlegm could start the team. Old Mike leaned his rifle against a beech, reached one hand under the sled, and when the jambock swung again, he pushed the sled, and boat, and all, nigh over steers and driver, to the top of a little rise, and sung out, "Stop, you d——d fool—always stop in a good place to begin."

I need not describe the times we had or the difficulties we overcame before we reached the river. We marched along, two each side the boat, with helping hands, should the steers get stuck. When I tell you that we passed deep swales, among big boulders in deep gorges, "breakneck hills," "Brandy Brook," and "Highwines Spring," you may conceive something of the obstacles and hindrances we met with. However, just before sundown, we cheered at sight of the river, and Otis and myself put forward to prepare supper. The old Oswegatchie looked good—looked like home. As the fire blazed up, Otis, full of cheer, began his "Hip, hip, and away she goes," etc., and the woods rang out the echoes. Just as we were about to call for supper, up came the steers, sweating, lolling, trembling, staggering. I gave the driver a phlegm cutter, and we all sat down to supper. After the day of toil, you may be sure provisions relished well, and Queen Victoria, or any other queen, was challenged to prepare such another repast as we made mouths at. We sat long and leisurely, all happy and thankful, light and joyous, save the driver. A panther had followed just in our wake through from the settlement, and, as it was fast growing dusky, the driver's apprehensions thickened that he and the steers might be intercepted in the dark. Truax said he didn't want to lose his sled, and so Old Mike advised the driver to take out the toggle, get on the nigh steer, and if the panther attacked him, to halloo "fire! murder! blood! and thunder!" and put the jambock to his *horned horses*. No sooner had he slipped the toggle than the steers took a hint of home, and away they went at a tearing canter, tails at an angle of forty-five. The last we saw of "mitten-mouth" he was pitching into the brush full tilt, bellowing and spitting "plug 'em"; and the last salutations he got from us were: "There they go!" "G—— d—— 'em!" "Run, you d——d fool!" "Hi! ye-e-e-e-a —ah!" . . .

Deer That Never Were Killed

The next morning early we got under way. After toiling ten miles up the river, among rocks, over rapids, sometimes neck deep in water, at three o'clock in the afternoon Old Mike, Otis, Truax, and myself entered the lake and with three cheers returned the salutations of a great buck that stood on a point just at its mouth. Our stores were soon got out, and we soon had supper under way. The outlet of the lake was to be our home shanty ground. We got a splendid view of the lake—nine miles long and four wide, interspersed with many islands and bounded by a succession of mountain peaks shrouded in perpetual blue. A thousand springs trickle down through rocky places with their cool contributions to old Cranberry, and when the winds blow strong and heavy it works and heaves with mighty pulsations and sends its waters down along its big artery to lave the soil for miles and miles. . . .

Think of knapsacks filled with pork, coarse rye and Indian, salt, onions, some coarse strong tea; think of big long knives in coat pockets; stout tin cups, dangling at each right side, and at the left a tin box or vessel, cartridge shaped, but twice as big and made to leak only at the top; a serviceable camp kettle and frying-pan cover and a chunked sheet-iron thing, with handle and spout; these latter shifting from one to another as the party get up to leave a spring or resting place. At the shanty, think of vast sheets of peeled bark, supported by poles and stakes over a big pile of hemlock boughs; light coarse woolen blankets depending, airing at the sides; a long clean sheet of spruce bark, inside up, with bread, salt, cups, whittled forks, long knives; on the pole across the fire a kettle of venison ribs and a chunk of pork boiling; on the coals, the pan sputtering with pork and trout and venison steak; beside the table, a jug of whiskey and a pot of onions.

The first night after our arrival at Cranberry we got a taste of the sport in store for us. After we had suppered, Truax sat with bared bootleg thrown over t'other, smoking quietly at the fire's corner; Old Mike was drawing up and pushing down his rifle wiper with evident good feeling; Otis had pitched into the woods to find a cedar and get timber for a paddle, and I lay with head resting on my hand beside the fire. As the sun went down, we talked of the journey we had come, of the immense and mountainous forest that lay between us and "sight of land" (said Old Mike), and the abundance of game that surrounded us. The wolves were beginning, one after another, their nightly concert, and we listened carelessly to their infernal discord. We had determined to hunt that night and were waiting for pitch dark. I took up the poker and, while punching at the fire, felt my fingers clinch round the stick, and I recovered from a sudden startle quick enough to get a thorough appreciation of a panther's voice.

The forked and tearing rattling of sound and shriek that fills the air when a panther screams makes the blood quicken and gives the muscles electric action. The veteran hunter starts his rifle from its resting place, attitudinizes, and never releases his chance grip of breech or barrel as long as there's hope of hearing—a rustle, a pipe-stem crack, or a foot put softly down among the leaves, giving note of whereabouts. 'Tis great luck to get a daylight shot at one of these lions of our forest. They are rarely seen by sunlight, unless when in some deep cove the watching hunter sees them reach their head and shoulders from the thick alders to lap water. When the panther finds himself discovered by human kind, he curls his great tail from side to side; his eyeballs dilate and stare with more of astonishment and curiosity than fear; and not until his eye takes the human contour and catches the human gaze does the panther shriek and hustle away. He seems to acquire a vast dread, and if perchance the rifle has not been deadly poised and break but a limb or make but a flesh-sore, he redoubles his efforts to get away with what strength he has remaining. If he makes a freezing screech or chance as he goes to bite a mouthful out of a spruce or hemlock, 'tis more from crazy dread than from anger.

But of the first hunt on Cranberry. As soon as it was pitch dark, Old Mike and I got our places in the canoe, he in the stern with the paddle, and I forward, just behind the standing jacklight. We expected tall sport. Just before sundown Truax had strolled up along the sand beach—at the lower end of which we shantied—and had reported an abundance of fresh spoor. But a few rods from where the boats were moored, Mike had shot a yearling doe by twilight and saw two others in the water near where she fell. Out we pushed, and I lit the wick. Within the area of our shanty noise, we expected no game and saw none. The jack threw a pale cast upon the shore, some four rods off, and the lofty forest that covered the bank looked shadowy. Clouds of flies rise up and stream in at the light from the thick blackness, in all directions, and sometimes put it nearly out. Millers—how significant the name to the night-hunter—come in large quantities, make tangents at the flame, whiff past it, and seem to clip off a part. There—one big miller has foundered in the grease, and he flaps and tumbles. "D——n the flies," involuntarily escapes me, and would escape a priest, as the light grows so dim that I cannot distinguish whether root or deer, twelve feet. "That d——d bat came near knocking out the flame"—whir-r-r-t, they go across my nose. The loons in the nooks in sight whistle out at our strange appearance, and a panther squalls out at us from a big bluff just ahead. Suddenly, my attention is diverted; flies, millers, bats, loons, and panther are forgotten as I spy out ahead, what, to one un-initiated, would have seemed pale rocks sticking up out of the water. I twist my body to the right and take up my rifle. The canoe moves on faster, for Old Mike has discovered what's ahead, and when the game's in sight the more speed the better. We approach within six rods. *There are fifteen or twenty deer within sight*—some a little startled, some watching with easy curiosity, most of them feeding quietly, unsuspiciously, so wonderful is the effect of the light upon them. Just before and nearest me stand three bucks and two does, side by side, facing the light. I draw a bead on the biggest buck and fire. Down he goes with a flounder, and souse! souse! splash! splash! the flock are in terrible affright and commotion. They jump all about us. A doe that was standing beside the buck dashes straight for the light, and I catch myself stooping to let her go over me; she veers, however, in her last jump and stands just beside me—*within six feet*. Old Mike's rifle breaks her down. Away go all the others up the bank, and 'twould have done your soul good to see the flitting flags as they crossed the water mark and disappeared among the norways [red pines]. "Venison, by ——," said Old Mike, and we set about reloading.

Our deer aboard, we went on. The air had freshened to a little breeze that blew right in our faces. The light flickered, so as to render it nearly useless, and I could, by turning the jack, barely keep it burning. We had not gone fifty rods from the first place of slaughter when I spied out just ahead in the edge of the rushes a young buck, feeding unconcernedly. I drew up and fired. "Missed him, by ——," whispered Old Mike. I heard a splashing and sousing, and by the time the smoke had cleared away, I had Mike's rifle to my face, and just as the buck was crossing the water mark I fired and broke him down. When the smoke again cleared, he lay kicking and making tremendous efforts to recover; he partly recovered, floundered about his length up the bank—recovered partly again, when I dropped my ramrod and rifle, pulled out my hatchet, jumped overboard, overtook him, and sank the hatchet to the eye just behind his ear. "Three dead deer," yes, said I, or soon will be. In short time we had him aboard, turned backs to the wind, and paddled for the shanty. Luck and future prospects animated us. The canoe moved swiftly, and we watched the tops of the tall norways to find our shanty ground. Old Mike felt good. Short, quick, animated expressions escaped him, such as "Fur Company, by ——"— "flock of deer"—"three great bucks"—"I b'lieve I won't go home"—"ha! h-a-a-a-a!" We soon landed at the shanty and swung up our venison. We had sound, refreshing sleep on the hemlock boughs and rose in the morning fresh and energetic. About sunrise Otis and Truax arrived from the head of the lake, where—I forgot to mention—they had gone the evening before. They had a great buck. Deer were very plenty there, but they had had "hunters' luck"—the unaccountable ill fortune which often follows the best concerted plans and most promising prospects.

Four deer were hanging by the noses near the beach, and after breakfast we prepared to skin and strip them. The meat of our deer, fit for that purpose, loaded our racks, and thick hardwood smoke enveloped it. It was being "jerked."

The night following 'twas rainy, and we couldn't hunt. Besides, a couple of panthers caterwauled all night on the sand beach, and Truax thought they kept the deer out of the water. The second morning at the lake, the sun rose warm and the sky was cloudless. We spent the forenoon shooting at a target. I wish I had measured the strings made by Old Mike, Truax, and Otis, at fifteen rods, off hand. They were—"some." . . .

After dinner Otis and Truax started in the skiff for the inlet of the lake, six miles up. The inlet—sometimes called the "Little River"—is from four to six rods wide and winds six miles through an immense beaver marsh, from three quarters to a mile wide. The inlet is from two to eight feet deep, weedy bottom in the shallow places, and its shores are lined, for the most part, with pond lilies. Here, fresh spoor is very abundant —lily pads nipped off, trampled down, turned over, and the mucky banks here and there are all cut up, and at every nook well-trod deer paths lead to the water. The immense flats on each side of the stream support tall grass and alders and here and there clumps of spiral spruce. In the summer and fall months, when the water is low, the surface of the flats lies about a foot above it and becomes hard and substantial. We couldn't step on shore without coming, every rod, on deer beds, most of them occupied the night before. You may conceive what a resort such a place must be for deer in hot fly-time and when feed has grown tough in the woods.

After Otis and Truax had got out of sight, I got into the canoe and thought I'd loiter along up the lake shore. You'd better believe a look at Cranberry in the afternoon of a hot day is interesting. I paddled along the winding shore with a pressing consciousness of the vast solitude about me, which the echoes from occasional taps of the paddle on the canoe side made stronger. The lake looked like molten silver; the sun shone hot upon it, and the green islands seemed to invite me to their grateful shade. Near its mouth the lake is narrow, and across it on the sand beach I count five deer, feeding in the water's edge. My attention was so much diverted that I didn't discover a deer that was standing in the grass just up a little cove until she blowed and started. I marked the place and thought I'd look sharp coming back. Bang! bang! I hear two rifles from Otis and Truax. Bang! again right after—three deer, thought I—*perhaps.*

I gave the canoe a couple of strokes out into the lake, threw in the paddle, slid myself down on the bottom, rested my head on the stern seat, and tried to snooze. I stood it but a few minutes—the sun made my bed almost an oven. I raised my head slowly to take a peep over the side. There was a doe feeding in the lily pads about fifty rods away. I stuck my rifle over the side and fired. She looked up, switched her tail, made a few dashes at the flies, and walked quietly up the bank. That's one of the does up here, thought I, that Truax tells about *never having been killed.* 'Twas time, perhaps, to catch a deer in the first-rate looking little cove where I started the one coming up, thought I, and so I reloaded and paddled down. As I rounded carefully the point which helped form the cove, I saw an immense buck standing belly deep in the water, up nearly sixty rods from me. He swung a lofty headdress and looked magnificent as the sun shone on him. I made no effort to get nearer. I might undoubtedly have approached within ten rods of him, for 'tis no uncommon thing to paddle within five rods of deer, in the daytime—paddling when their heads are down to feed. They freeze when they look up. I had a new patent rifle, so I drew it to my face and fired. The buck looked up, straight at me, as much as to say, who the devil are you? That's one of the bucks up here, thought I, that never was killed. But I was unaccustomed to my rifle; besides, it had never been sighted accurately—and I thought these facts some apology for missing. After reloading, I paddled leisurely for home. I passed a deer to the left, about eighty rods off, having determined to shoot no more until I had fixed and marked my sights. When opposite the sand beach across the lake, where I had seen deer when I went up, I saw there were ten or a dozen in the water. I stopped to look.

A dozen deer in the water's edge within the space of half a mile, some feeding quietly, others cutting antics, make to the sportsman a pleasing, thrilling spectacle. A thought struck me: where's Old Mike? I left him at the shanty, but he's off in some other direction. This had just run through my brain when—up went all the flags *but one,* and out went every deer *but one,* and then I heard a rifle. Down along the bank about seventy rods, I saw a thin blue smoke and, beneath the vapor, Old Mike reloading. I sent up an Indian yell and paddled stiff across the lake. Across, I found a fine young buck, hauled him into the canoe, and paddled home.

The next morning, just after daylight, Otis and Truax came down the lake with three deer, one buck and two does. In short time we had their skins off and their meat in brine. During the day we sported ourselves fishing trout and shooting *at* loons. Old Mike killed a doe that stuck her head out of the alders just across the river from where he was fishing. The night following, we heard thunder rumbling off towards the north and seemingly beneath us. We got everything we could pick up, under cover, and the storm came on.

In perfect security we enjoyed the violence and sublimity of a thunder storm in rocky highlands. A loud roar came from the lake as the heavy drops of rain fell upon it. We saw the lightning-serpents darting down the sky, illuminating the woods with a pale light, which showed us the tall trees, spectre-like, and

> From peak to peak, the rattling crags among,
> Leaps the live thunder!

At gray in the morning we all turned out. The sky was cloudless, and we saw over the peaks eastwardly that the sun was coming up with warmth and glory. The lake was completely covered with bubbles, which looked like little globules of silver. As the sun rose up, the mist from the wet woods enveloped the mountain peaks, reminding one of Ossian's "ghost of the hills, which moves upon the sunbeam." The little globules burst in the sunshine, and by ten o'clock the surface moisture had dried up. The spring that ran past our shanty was swollen considerably, and the water was distasteful. Speaking of swelling reminds me of a little bit of fun made that morning. Old Mike's rifle wiper had lain outside during the night and was so swollen by the rain that it wouldn't enter the bore. After attempting to use it, he laid his rifle over a stump with the wiper just sticking in the muzzle, walked off, and sat down —"I'll go home," said he; *"my rifle's shrunk."*

Our jerking racks were already loaded with a second load of venison, and duty, conscience, every *human* consideration, forbade an indiscriminate, unrelenting havoc. We had nearly all the meat we wanted or could take out of the woods with us, so we determined to relax our energy after deer and enjoy "life in the woods," carelessly, leisurely. Old Mike said he was going to kill a catapainter and started off. Otis and myself spent most of the day at the shanty, jerking venison. Towards night Old Mike got back. He had a nice string of brook trout, the tenderloins of two deer, and three partridges. Otis and myself immediately set about cleaning the varieties of game, while Old Mike talked to me about what he had heard and what he had seen of game and timber and country. Before dark we had the camp kettle filled with prepared ingredients for a grand chowder next day noon. Old Mike had stepped down to the lake to secure the boats for the night and, when coming back, discovered that one of his tracks made in the sand going down had been put out by the paw of a panther. All hands were called to look.

At about two o'clock next day, Otis flipped the cover off the kettle and—ye gods, what a dish—how rich, how delicious—good for sore eyes, intoxicating to the olfactories. Here and there stuck up, out of the rich simmering gravy, the white breast of a partridge, ends of venison ribs; and bits of rich red trout and little flakes of pork floated on top. We danced, yelled, improvisated, imprecated, and hurried at it. "God bless the rich, the poor can beg," said Old Mike. But your mouth waters, and so *nuf ced* 'bout the chowder.

The next morning we skinned and stripped a very fine buck, which Old Mike had killed the evening before, and after breakfast he and Otis got ready and put off up the lake to explore its head and the inlet. I spent the day, or most of it, curing venison and target shooting and towards sundown caught some trout. As the sun went below the horizon, I saw black heavy masses of cloud heaving up to northward, and during the night there was another thunderstorm. I lay securely in the shanty, thinking often of the boys at the head of the lake—what a soaking they will get. However, the sun rose warm next morning. Just as I had breakfast ready, I heard Otis and Old Mike land on the beach, and I went down. They looked as if they had been hauled through the lake. Otis hurried up to the shanty and pitched at the alcohol. They had killed two deer—one going up the day before and one coming down that morning. After breakfast they lay down to nap, and I set to work to strip their venison. About ten o'clock Truax arrived. He had come to stay with us the rest of the campaign.

Gull Rock

The rock was known to "Bowles" as Gull Island before the dam submerged its base. The acorn-shaped top is still prominent. (Photo by Dwight Church)

The next two or three days we spent paddling carelessly about the lake with our rifles and with fishing tackle in our pockets; occasionally bowling over a venison and, when we came to trout holes, dropping in our hooks. Friday afternoon 'twas still, warm, and cloudy. It promised to be a fine night for hunting, so Otis and myself, having determined to have a night's hunt on the inlet before we left, jumped into the canoe and put off up the lake. About a mile [away], just off the mouth of the inlet, lies Gull Island—a bed of broken sandstone. In the middle of the island an immense rock, acorn shaped, rises up some twenty-five feet high and is about fifteen feet in diameter; it would make you think of the earliest time, and how the waters of the deluge must have dashed and eddied around it. A cloud of gulls stay and hover about and above it. Its sides are whitened with guano, and at any hour in the day a large white one, of the gull species, may be seen on its summit peak. As we approached the rock, the gulls got into terrible commotion, and Otis was determined to land and examine the island. As he stepped out of the canoe, her bow lifted off the stones, and I backed off to get a sort of perspective, for Otis said he was going to climb to the top of the rock. He piles stones, one above another, all heedless of the passes the birds were making at him, and after getting to the height of about ten feet, he managed to stick on to and crawl up the side to the apex. Without hat or coat, vest unbuttoned, bosom open, one trouser leg tucked into the top of his boot, hair down over his eyes, tobacco juice coloring his chin—he swings and balances on the sharp point; makes a fling with one hand forward, the other backward, then sideways, as the gulls make dashes at him, whiff past his head—cu-r-r-k! cu-r-r-k!—and reach down their legs, as if to twist their toes into his sorrel hair. He descends, and a sort of triumphant murmur comes from the gulls as they begin to rise higher. There were several old nests near the apex of the rock, in the little hollows and crevices, and a great many among the stones on the island. We moved off from the island amidst the clamorous congratulations of the white-winged messengers we had disturbed.

We soon entered the mouth of the inlet and began to look out for venison. We got one shot before it grew dark. We both missed. 'Twas a fair shot—broadside, at about fifteen rods—a big doe, standing just in the edge of the water. "Mum! mum!" as if nothing had happened—we never looked at each other, never spoke, and not a word has passed between us about that shot to this day. 'Twas evident, as it grew towards evening, that the fates were against us, for the sky brightened up, and the moon showed her full face in the east. Our hunting that night was up. We paddled up the inlet about a mile, went ashore, and fixed ourselves for a night's sleep. We thought we would stay and try to get some shots going home in the gray of morning. We built a fire and lay down at the roots of a big hemlock. When just about to fall asleep, Otis rustled and raised up on his elbow—"That's the same litter of wolves I heard the other night," said he. It was a yelling, yelping, like what a litter of a dozen puppies would make. Otis rigged his lantern and put off in the direction of the noise. I fell away beside my rifle and was soon asleep. Just before gray of morning I awoke refreshed, poked up the fire, and while making my breakfast of a piece of jerked venison, a hard biscuit, and a little whiskey and water—thinking all the time, "Where the devil's Otis?"—I heard two rifle cracks down about two miles on the lake shore. I recognized Otis's signal and put down for him. While paddling along the inlet, I came upon and killed a small doe. Otis answered my rifle, and when I had reloaded and got my deer aboard, I shipped the oars and pulled strong for him. He hailed me from the shore, and I turned in.

"Where's your wolves?"

"D——n the wolves! they stopped yelping. I've hunted the woods back here all over and can't find a d——d one on 'em."

"How came your face scratched and your breeches torn?"

"D——n the briars! d——n the rocks! they liked to perish me."

As I brought the canoe alongside, Otis reached out one boot into it, and I saw the upper was torn up.

"How'd ye tear yer boot?"

"T' other's worse 'an that," said he, as he pulled it out of the weeds into the canoe, the sole hanging by the heel and tied with moosewood bark up over the instep.

"Ha! ha! ha! you're a picture for a painter!"

"D——n the wolves!"

We laid our course straight through the middle of the lake and in the space of an hour arrived at the shanty.

The following afternoon we were to leave the lake, and Old Mike and Truax had nearly all our traps in readiness when we arrived. We had some venison still on the racks and some unpeeled, but we determined to hurry up the smoke as much as possible, so that we might bag what was already over the fire, and to leave what of the fresh we couldn't eat in the skin, for whatever of the carnivorous might chance along.

We counted game. We had killed *and got,* since we entered the lake—nine days—*eighteen deer.* We had cured six or seven of the best skins taken off. 'Twas out of season for trout fishing, and we made no effort to kill more than we wanted to eat. We could at any time kill as many as would fill our big frying pan. We had made no effort to take any of the larger game, such as wolf, bear, and panther, though we were satisfied we might have succeeded. We regretted very much that we had not a rare specimen to grace our return to civilized domain.

After we had partaken of a sumptuous dinner, we shouldered our rifles and left the shanty. Our traps and venison all packed into our large boat, we jumped in and shoved her from the sand beach. As we neared the mouth of the lake, we rose up and roared out of "brazen throats," from "adamantine lungs," *three times three*. Down went our craft through the swift, narrow outlet, and when we turned our heads to look back, we were below the lake's surface, and in another moment we doubled a point that concealed the opening from us.

It seemed like leaving loved and enticing home to quit old Cranberry. All day long, while struggling with the rapid current, in the water waist deep, we felt regret and thought and talked of its water, its islands, its horizon—all its gorgeous scenery.

Truax killed a great buck on the river the night following, and we jerked his meat at our next shanty fire. Nineteen deer we then counted, and so determined to hunt no more.

After three days' toil we reached the settlement in Fine, and the morning following our arrival there, before the day had dawned, we piled into our vehicle, and by sundown we had whirled along over fifty miles of road, rough and smooth, to the mouth of the river whose source had been to us the scene of glorious pastime. . . .

BOWLES

Ogdensburgh, N.Y.

CHAPTER II

The Great Windfall

ALBERT FOWLER

THE WINDFALL took place seven years before Bowles and his friends worked their way up the Oswegatchie to Cranberry Lake, and they must have crossed the broad swath of downed and tangled timber as they passed between Buck Mountain and Cook Pond. From their position on the river they saw only a small segment, however, and were probably unaware of the magnitude of the destruction. At any rate, Bowles does not mention the Windfall.

Aside from one or two hunters who reported being within hearing distance, no witnesses are known to have observed the storm when it struck in the Cranberry Lake region. There were no residents in the area at the time. The nearest communities from which we have firsthand accounts are Fowler and Edwards, some twenty miles to the west.

The first part of this chapter, which appeared originally in *Weatherwise* (August, 1961), is a short history of the immense storm or series of storms which swept across New York State from Niagara Falls to Plattsburgh in 1845, leaving tornado wreckage and windfall in its wake. Next comes a series a eyewitness accounts from contemporary newspapers. Several of these are quoted from clippings in the William C. Redfield Papers in the Sterling Library, Yale University. Redfield's interest in the Adirondacks was aroused when in 1837, as meteorologist, he joined the party of scientists and others that made the first recorded ascent of Mount Marcy. The chapter closes with descriptions of the Cranberry section of the Windfall as it was after fire or decay had laid it open for settlement, and as it is today.

On the afternoon and evening of September 20, 1845, four unusual events took place over northern New York State in this sequence:

1. A tornado swept through parts of Niagara and Orleans

counties on the southwest shore of Lake Ontario about noon and then passed out into the lake.

ALBERT FOWLER

2. A seiche, or sudden rise and fall of the water level, was noticed along both the United States and Canadian shores. At Cobourg, Ontario, observers attributed the phenomenon to a violent earthquake.

3. During the afternoon one or more tornadoes raced across the Adirondacks from the vicinity of Watertown to Lake Champlain, passing just north of Cranberry Lake, Tupper Lake, Upper Saranac Lake, and Lake Placid.

4. A series of severe thunderstorms hit the Mohawk Valley in central New York, with brilliant displays of lightning visible at dusk in western Vermont.

All of these events seem to have been connected with the same unstable atmospheric conditions attending the passage of a squall line and cold front. The tornado in Orleans and Niagara counties may well have moved east-northeast across the lake as a waterspout, lifted for a while, and then struck again northeast of Watertown. Its agitation of the lake waters could have caused the remarkable rise and fall of the water level. The turbulent conditions attending the squall line could easily have triggered the thunderstorms observed to the southward and eastward that afternoon and evening.

The first tornado damage was reported near Johnson Creek in Niagara County northeast of Buffalo. From there the vortex cut a path northeastward, three-quarters of a mile wide and about twenty miles long, through the communities of Yates and Carlton in Orleans County, where buildings, orchards, and forests were destroyed. It passed out into Lake Ontario at the mouth of Oak Orchard Creek northwest of Rochester, endangering the steamboat *Express* on its regular run. The funnel seems not to have been observed from either shore, but a large waterspout was reported from the middle of the lake, together with hail and thunderstorms.

Chester Dewey, professor of natural history at the Rochester Collegiate Institute, made a study of the rise and fall of the water that afternoon. At the mouth of the Genesee River the water suddenly moved out, leaving the harbor with its bays and coves exposed. Ten or twelve minutes later the water returned to a higher level than before, and this oscillation was repeated several times. The fall was two feet below normal, and the rise two feet above normal. The same fluctuation was observed on the Canadian shore at Cobourg, where it continued from noon until dusk. At Oswego a large mass of floating logs swirled out of the harbor and then rushed back in again on the returning wave.

The tornado, apparently exhibiting a skipping action, struck well inland from the lake shore northeast of Watertown. The first damage reported here came at Antwerp, about ten miles north of the present Camp Drum military reservation and some thirty-five miles inland in northeastern Jefferson County. The path of the twister then took a course through southern St. Lawrence County, where it flattened over four thousand acres of timber in the town of Fowler and six thousand acres of timber in the town of Edwards. Its swath was reported to be three-quarters of a mile wide in Fowler. After traveling eight miles, it widened to one and a half miles in Edwards. This eight-mile stretch, swept clean of every tree and building, was thought to be part of a forty-mile swath running through the rural communities of Fowler and Edwards to Russell on the north and touching Pitcairn and Fine to the south.

Some fifteen miles southeast of the town of Russell appeared a second swath, which came to be known as the Great Windfall of 1845 on maps of St. Lawrence County. It was a half-mile wide stretch from a point just north of Cranberry Lake to the eastern boundary of the county. A close study of the quadrangle maps of the United States Geological Survey shows evidence that this swath extended another five miles east into Franklin County to the vicinity of Derrick. The evidence is a Windfall Pond and a Windfall Brook in Franklin County on the same east-northeast bearing as two features with identical names in St. Lawrence County.

For the next thirty miles of forests, lakes, and mountains

there are no reports of tornado activity that can be traced to-day. But a tornado emerged from the wilderness at Union Falls in Essex County on the same compass line as the Great Windfall. Farther along the same line, buildings in the town of Peru were damaged. Slightly to the south of this track some damage occurred in the villages of Wilmington and Keeseville, and out on Lake Champlain a whirlwind pried up several loose deck planks from the steamer *Burlington* that were later found miles away. In the northern part of the city of Burlington on the Vermont shore some buildings suffered minor wind damage. Whether the Wilmington-Keeseville-Burlington line was a third tornado or the continuance of one of the two major windfalls previously described cannot be determined at this late date.

The airline distance from Johnson Creek in western New York to Burlington is approximately 275 miles. If the track had been continuous at the surface of the ground, it would have closely approached the record attributed to the Mattoon, Illinois, tornado in 1917, which traveled 293 miles.

Many people had miraculous escapes from serious injury and death, but in the whole course of destruction no fatalities were laid directly to the storm, though a woman and child were said to have disappeared at the mouth of Oak Orchard Creek near Carlton. The speed of the twister was estimated as high as fifty miles an hour. The seiche was first observed at Cobourg shortly before noon, and it was reported that a tornado struck Antwerp at 3 P.M., Union Falls at 5 P.M., and Burlington at 6 P.M. If the storm covered the 115 miles between Antwerp and Burlington in three hours, it was averaging just under forty miles an hour, and at this rate it must have first visited Johnson Creek at about 11:30 A.M. and been in line with Cobourg about noon, with Rochester shortly before 1 P.M., with Oswego around 2 P.M., and with Cranberry Lake just before 4 P.M.

These are the bare facts of the storm as they can be pieced together from contemporary records and careful research into a period before the beginning of the Weather Bureau's published records in 1871. More interesting are the firsthand accounts of wreckage and windfall, of human belongings and houses and barns sucked into the sky, and of people who lived through the storm and told their stories of danger and damage.

Their reports follow, beginning with the Fowler-Edwards area where the destruction was heaviest, extending to the Lake Champlain region, and returning to concentrate on the only enduring relic of the tornado's havoc, the Great Windfall just north of Cranberry Lake.

Z. H. Benton, of Fullerville, owned an iron works bordering the tornado track, and his close examination of the damage forms the basis of the report in the Watertown *Jeffersonian,* as reprinted in the New York *Municipal Gazette* of March 2, 1846:

An awfully destructive and appalling tornado passed over a part of Jefferson, St. Lawrence, and Essex counties on the 20th inst., which so far as we can learn, has no parallel in this region of country. We have been favored by Z. H. Benton, Esq., whose iron works are situated about one hundred and fifty rods from the north line of the track, which embraces eight miles of the action of the tornado in the towns of Fowler and Edwards, St. Lawrence County, and we have reports of its progress nearly one hundred miles from where it first struck the earth. The tornado first commenced its work of destruction about one mile east of Antwerp village, in this county, and its track, when it reached the adjoining town of Fowler, was three-fourths of a mile wide, increasing to a mile and a half wide in the course of eight miles—covering four thousand acres in Fowler and six thousand in the town of Edwards. In all the distance there is not a tree nor a building of any description left standing; all were prostrated by its mighty force, leaving widespread ruin and desolation as evidence of its power.

Embraced in this distance, situated on the Pitcairn Road and another passing parallel through Emmerson's and Streeter's settlements, some two miles apart, were sixteen buildings, dwellings, barns, and one schoolhouse, every one of which was instantly swept away as with the besom of destruction; but, strange as it may appear, no lives were lost, nor were any very seriously injured! This will appear the more extraordinary when we state particulars. Large

ALBERT
FOWLER

trees and roofs of buildings, boards, hay, grain, &c. &c., were carried and whirled about in the air like straws and twigs in a whirlpool, presenting an awfully sublime and appalling sight. Large and well cultivated farms are covered with trees and the wrecks of forests so that the labor and expense of clearing is estimated to be greater than when said farms were in a state of nature. The tornado first struck Antwerp at about 3 P.M. and travelled at the rate of about fifty miles per hour. It is reported that after leaving St. Lawrence County and crossing the great forest lying between Black River and Lake Champlain, it struck a new village and extensive iron works near Keeseville, Essex County, which it entirely destroyed.

We have room only for a few particulars; but these, strange as they may appear, may be relied on as substantially correct. Our informant, Mr. Benton, . . . has examined the ground with a view to the facts alone, and his statement is entitled to the most implicit belief. . . .

Among the things carried away from this settlement [Emmerson and Streeter] was a feather bed, since found in what is called "Pond's Settlement," sixteen miles distant!

Crossing the Oswegatchie, the next settlement in line of the tempest was the Pitcairn Road, embracing ten buildings. Near the north line of the tornado, among the sufferers was a Mr. Brown, who had recently erected a large forty by thirty feet barn, which he had filled with the products of his farm. This, with his house, was blown down and the contents scattered far and wide. Mr. B. was taken up and carried fifteen or twenty rods, unconscious of the moving power, and was severely bruised upon the head, shoulders, and other parts of his body. When he struck the ground he seized hold of a stump and by that means saved himself from further personal injury. His family in the house took refuge in the cellar and were thus saved. The next house south of Mr. B. was that of Mr. Leonard, in which were two women and five children. Hearing the noise of the tornado and seeing its approach, these also took refuge in the cellar. One of the women last descending was struck by the timbers of the house and rendered senseless, in which condition she remained nearly a day. It is said that she will ultimately recover. Next to Mr. Leonard's stood another house—the name of the occupant not given—in which was a sick woman with a young child about three weeks old and a young woman named Kinney, who was attending upon her. Frightened by the noise and looks of the tempest as it approached, Miss K. threw herself upon another bed in the same room, when the house was blown down and one of the logs of which it was composed fell across the bed of Miss K. and held the latter fast. The sick woman immediately rose from her bed and by almost superhuman strength removed the log and thus saved the life of the young lady!

Near the latter house, in the street, was a man driving a yoke of oxen attached to a wagon laden with coal, being from sixty to eighty rods distant from any standing trees. Two large trees were brought by the wind and laid across the wagon, crushing it without injury to the team or to the man, except the tearing of his clothes and slight scratches of his person. The team was so bound in by the trees and rubbish that it required several hours to extricate them, which was not effected until the Monday following. [The storm occurred on a Saturday.]

A frame schoolhouse standing near Mr. Brown's dwelling, in which were several children and their teacher, was moved entire from its foundation without injury to its inmates. A hemlock tree, said to be from two to two and a half feet in diameter, standing on the west side of the Oswegatchie, was taken up whole and deposited on the coal job on the east side of the river, distant two miles! A log schoolhouse in the town of Edwards was taken over the heads of the scholars—every log, down to those on which the floor timbers rested, carried away without injury to its inmates.

The village of Fullerville is situated on the Oswegatchie, about one hundred and fifty rods distant from the north line of the tornado. Its citizens had a full view of the storm as it passed and were consequently enabled to judge of its force and appearance. At this place, although out of the track, its force was perceptibly felt. A grist mill, the timbers of which in the lower story are from twenty inches to two feet square, rocked to its foundation.

Immediately following the tornado was a storm of hail, some of the stones as large as hen's eggs, severely lacerating the cattle exposed, as they fell.

We have thus briefly described the effects of the storm in eight miles of its length; we are not in possession of sufficient data to state accurately its effects after it left Benton and Fine's Tract, in the town of Edwards. But as the great eastern forest borders on the latter line, it is not probable that any considerable damage was done, except to standing timber, until it reached the inhabited parts of Essex County.

ALBERT
FOWLER

A briefer on-the-spot report of the tornado from Essex County is contained in the following item from the Plattsburgh *Republican,* reprinted in the same issue of the New York *Municipal Gazette* of March 2, 1846:

At Union Falls, in this county, it emerged from the forest, making a complete wreck of many of the buildings in that place, and for a distance of twenty miles in a northeasterly direction, over a tract from eight to one hundred rods in width, it swept everything before it—trees, fences, barns, and houses were leveled with the ground. Duncan's forge was considerably injured, the chimneys blown off even with the roof, and several outbuildings destroyed. The brick schoolhouse near the Travis forge in Peru was utterly demolished, and the brick dwelling of H. N. Peabody, nearby, was partially destroyed. We hear of two houses that were blown down over the heads of the inmates, and it is most extraordinary that no lives were lost. Some fifteen or twenty buildings were destroyed or injured in that vicinity by the wind, which committed no further depredations until it reached Burlington, where it unroofed the house of Mr. Moody, blew down some barns, etc. It struck the steamer *Burlington* near Fort Cassin, but she braved the storm handsomely, suffering no greater damage than the loss of some loose deck planks, which were picked up miles from the shore.

An extract from a letter dated Shoreham, Vermont, October 13, 1845, from Clark Rich to Eben Meriam, is quoted in the dispatch from the Plattsburgh *Republican* to show another aspect of the storm:

On the evening of the 20th of September we had the most majestic display of lightning I ever saw. Many other elderly people say so. The upper part of a dense cloud, coming slowly from the northwest, was almost constantly lighted up with flashes and spangled streaks shooting in every direction, upwards as often as otherwise. Occasionally the lightning would streak to the ground. As it approached, the thunder commenced its roar and increased without intermission until it passed by me. Just before the rain commenced, there was a narrow black cloud directly over me, so dense that I could not see the lightning through it, but the light from the flashes was very vivid on each side of the cloud. The beauty of the scenery was before and after the shower passed. The latter I did not notice.

Another clipping in the Redfield files, from the New York *Commercial Advertiser* of September 24, 1845, quotes an unnamed correspondent who wrote from Burlington on the day of the storm:

This town was visited, this evening, by the most grand and awful storm of thunder, lightning, rain, and wind that we have ever experienced.

The wind during the day was south, but toward night it veered around to the east, and so on to the north and northwest; the clouds gathered blackness, and on the lake to the NW, the appearance was like the premonitory symptoms of a storm at sea. At dusk, the horizon in the west from south to north and so around to the east was alternately, with the rapidity of thought, a blaze of fire or a sheet of blackness, dark as midnight.

In the distance could be heard the roaring as of mighty waters. Onward, fitful and furious, came the raging blast; trees are leveled to the ground, chimneys demolished, barns and houses unroofed; the fragments flying all around show the power and fury of the storm. The rain descends in very torrents. The balustrade and the chimneys on Messrs. Strong's store (formerly the Burlington Hotel) and the chimneys on Messrs. Peck's store, are swept off clean to the roof.

The roof of Mr. John Bradley's new brick barn was entirely blown off and the building nearly demolished. Mrs. Doctor Moody's fine dwelling, near the female seminary, had the roof entirely taken off, and the storm of wind and rain poured in upon the terrified inmates; the house and everything in it were completely drenched.

This *is* something new for Burlington. I have not heard as yet of further damages.

The steamer *Burlington* left the wharf a short time before the blow—in time, I judge, to get into Shelburne Bay, or over to the other shore, before the storm.

An undated report on "The Gale of the 20th Sept." in the Utica *Gazette* shows that the storm was felt as far south as the Mohawk Valley and stirred up interest about its effects elsewhere:

A counterpart to the storm which was felt with such severity in this neighborhood appears to have occurred on the afternoon of the

same day, in St. Lawrence County, passing through the towns of
Fine, Russell, Edwards, and Fowler, passing within one hundred
and fifty rods of the village of Fullerville. It took, says the Ogdensburgh *Sentinel,* a southwesterly direction in a track forty miles long,
varying from one mile to sixty rods in width, tearing off branches
from the largest trees, and mingling them at the height of sixty feet
in the air, with hay and grain, fowls, beds, bedding and clothing of
every description, taken from the houses which the fury of the elements had overthrown. Whole stacks of hay and grain and house-
hold furniture were blown from one-half to three-quarters of a mile
into the woods and destroyed. The tempest continued about ten
minutes, passing off with a torrent of rain.

A Mr. Cole and wife and child were sitting in a log house; the
whole house from the bottom log was carried from them, passing
over their heads, without injuring them.

From Cranberry Lake to Peru, a distance of seventy
miles as the crow flies, the tornado appears to have traveled in
a relatively straight line, forty miles of which can be pretty
accurately traced by windfall and swath according to records
and research. It is the first twenty miles of that track, known
locally as the Windfall, which is of particular interest to the
historian because of the great fire that cleared out the downed
timber and left its traces in the area for more than a century.

In a passage from *The Forest Arcadia of Northern New
York,* published in 1864, the author, Nathaniel Wheeler Coffin, describes the Windfall north of Cranberry Lake and states
that a great fire had swept through the area before that date:

After much hard travel, and a few falls, we at length saw
through the gloom of the forest, the opening of the great windfall,
which, under the burning rays of a meridian sun, contrasted with the
darkness of the woods upon its borders, shone like a band of gold.
Proceeding beyond the well-defined edge of the wood and ascending
a little knoll, we were enabled to observe and enjoy the beauty of
the landscape. On our right the Oswegatchie River rolled darkly
and rapidly. In front Cranberry Hill [Bear Mountain?] and the
highlands upon the shores of the lake, which lay two miles beyond,
loomed up in the distance. On our left the broad savannah of the
windfall, bare of trees and covered with wild grasses, rose and fell,
as far as the eye could reach, in graceful undulations.

My curiosity was greatly excited to know something more about this windfall than I had yet heard. "What is the history of this windfall?" I asked the squire [an unidentified leading citizen of Russell, possibly Julius M. Palmer].

"It is the effect of one of the most remarkable tornadoes that ever visited this continent, I apprehend," he replied. . . . "You can imagine, but it is impossible for me to describe . . . the appearance of this mass of timber as I first saw it not long afterwards; every tree, great and small, within the line of its course, taken up by the roots and thrown together in the most unutterable confusion and piled in some places to the height of the tallest trees left standing upon its margin."

"You say this occurred in 1845. How is it that this great convulsion has left so few marks behind it? I should have expected to see the ground covered with the dead trunks and roots of the trees, but on the contrary it is as clear as a prairie and as blooming as a young widow just gone into colors."

"In course of time," he replied, "the timber became dry; lying across the track of the hunter on his journey to the lake and the streams beyond, it presented a most vexatious obstruction. Doubtless some selfish person of this class, reckless of the injury he might do to the property of another, on which he was pursuing his unlicensed sport, yielded to the temptation presented by the combustible condition of the branches and set it on fire. The principle of decay has done the rest. There are a few of the old logs left. Here is one of them," said he, kicking his foot against a charred stump, "but there are not many."

"What is in the way of ploughing up the windfall and planting it, or laying it down to grass?" I asked.

"Nothing," he replied. "You may run a plough for miles along the clearing, even into Jamestown and Piercefield, without striking a rock, and as to the quality of the soil, dig in it as deep as you like, and you will find it a series of layers of decayed vegetation, the waste of, who knows how many, successions of forests since the beginning of creation."

Thirty years after Coffin's visit the Forest Commission of the state, in its annual report for 1893, found the track of the Windfall still plainly discernible, though in many places overgrown with young trees. It suggested, however, that the account of a fire might be erroneous:

The Henry M. Clark Farm in 1920

Situated near the Grass River a half mile south of the Windfall, the farm once had Windfall, New York, as its post-office address. The original log house (*at right*) was built in 1878 and is still in use today. From 1884 until 1922, it was the home of the Clarks and their nine children. The two children on the lawn are grandsons. (Photo by Paul J. Smith)

Bill MacAleese's Hotel on the Windfall, about 1915

Occupied by MacAleese until the end of the 19th century, the hotel was patronized by loggers, hunters and fishermen. (Courtesy Mrs. Clara McKenney)

A special examination of this strip of land was made recently by the forester in charge of that district, who reports that the old track is thickly overgrown with poplar; and that the poplar growing there is the largest and healthiest he has seen, the greater part of the trees exceeding eighteen inches in diameter. In no other place in the Great Forest has the second-growth poplar which succeeded a fire attained a diameter of ten inches.

It may be that, contrary to Mr. Coffin's supposition, the fallen timber was not burned, but perished by decay; in which case the vigorous condition of the present growth is easily accounted for.

The western end of the Windfall was a tempting prospect for settlement. The land had been cleared by tornado and by fire or decay and appeared suitable for farming. Fish and game were plentiful for food, and sportsmen occasionally needed board and lodging. Ivan Bancroft, who grew up in the area, tells how it was settled shortly after the Civil War by his family and other hardy pioneers:

At the western end of the eight-mile strip of windfall that I was familiar with John Cook tried to establish a farm. The soil was not very productive, but Mr. Cook stayed on, living by hunting, fishing, and a little guiding. The location came to be known as Cook's Corners, and the old farm today is as barren as it was in 1870.

From Cook's eastward for five or six miles the land was very barren. A few willows grew along the streams, some tangles of wild raspberries and blackberries with now and then a few stunted aspens. In a few places tamarack trees had grown to a fair size but had been killed off by a blight about the time of my birth in 1892. The rest of the land was mostly rocky, barren, hilly country. In some places moss and paintbrush covered the otherwise bare soil. A few places had some sparse grass.

In the late 1870's a Mr. Berkley had a lumber camp at the edge of the Windfall, about five miles from Cook's and near the Grass River. About a mile from Berkley's on the north side of the river another farm was attempted by a family named Irish. The farm was a failure and Irish was gone long before my time.

About two miles farther east were two other families, Charles Downer and Richard Bullock. Bullock's place was probably the first house around there and was to the best of my knowledge built shortly after the Civil War. I was able to pick out the ruins of its cellar in the summer of 1961. Neither family was successful at farming. The land, along with the Irish farm, is still bare except for some spots where the State Conservation Department has done some reforestation. The pines it planted seem to do well in the sandy soil, and the territory is hardly recognizable now.

ALBERT
FOWLER

The tornado strip was not continuous. The wind would clear everything from its path for several miles and then skip for a few miles. From those farms eastward for about three miles was a skipped place. It was, in spite of much lumbering, heavily timbered. At the end of that was the house of Preston Shurtleff. Much of his clearing is still bare, although the young forest is beginning to cover it. A few miles more of windfall, and we come to Seavey's [now Sevey's]. There is still a hotel of sorts at Seavey's Corners. [It was called the Windfall House on early maps, a name recently re-adopted.] Much of the nearby land is covered only by second growth evergreens.

The people I have mentioned were or had been living there when in 1878 my grandfather, John R. Mills, and my father, George Bancroft, went to a location about a half mile from the Windfall and about a mile from the Downer farm, at a place called Owens Plains. Near the Plains they hewed logs and built a log house. My father took his family to Cranberry Lake, and my mother's sister and family (the Henry Clarks) lived on the old farm and raised nine children. They attended school along with the Downer children in a log schoolhouse near the Bullock farm. The original log house is still standing and still in use. It is the main building at a resort hotel or motel about two and a half miles from Cranberry Lake and is called Rustic Lodge.

Mr. Mills helped to build the first dam at Cranberry Lake and later had a small sawmill at what is now called the Old Forge. My father first went to Cranberry Lake about 1875. He was a pretty fair carpenter and helped to build Tramps Retreat and the Vann cottage on Buck Island. He was cook and guide for Fred Howlett for many years, and as a little kid I spent several summers at Tramps Retreat along with Ames Howlett and the Durston boys.

There is no evidence any more of the fire, and so far as I know there is no record of the time of the fire. I have heard many tales of it, and when I was a small boy there were some charred stumps and occasionally the moss-covered remains of a tree. My best guess would be that the fire followed the slash by only a few years, possibly only one or two. It is also quite likely that only this one area burned at that time.

Bill MacAleese lived in the Windfall near where the Grass River crosses it.

Some of the settlers on the Windfall found a means of support in taking hunters as guests. In the early 1890's there were three such "hotels"—Cook's, the Thomas House, and the Windfall House. A little later the MacAleese place on the Grass River became a mecca for hunters and a clearing house for stories about the great storm of 1845. The following story, as reported by the *St. Lawrence Plaindealer* of Canton, March 15, 1921, was told by Bill MacAleese himself and concerned a woodsman he knew, "Old Ben Downer":

The day the wind and things blew, Ben was going north to Granshue [in the vicinity of South Colton], and he heard a terrific roaring, but it was at a distance, and the forest through which he was traveling prevented his seeing any of the sky except directly overhead. He didn't know what was happening, but he did know that whatever it was it was big. There was a great deal of lightning and terrific thunder but no rain, he used to say.

After a time he got to what has ever since been known as the Windfall, and he knew instantly what had happened. He struck a solid wall. The trees were twisted and torn. Huge forest monarchs looked as though some giant hand had seized them from above and twisted them around and around until they had been twisted apart. The tangle was terrific. Ben went hither and yon trying to find a place to get through and finally gave it up and decided the only thing to do was to strike a straight line and crawl and climb and hack and hew his way through. It took him a solid day to get through the slash, and he slept out that night.

Vira H. Phelps, the daughter of Willard Howland, looks back on the Windfall as she first saw it around 1890:

The first I remember about the Windfall is that it was covered with dead trees and blueberries. The Bullocks were living there and also the Henry Clarks. A family by the name of Stewart were on the Company farm [Canton Lumber Company's farm near the Grass River]. Later on MacAleese lived there.

At the time I remember it, people came from everywhere for blueberries. They took bushels away and used to go there and camp for days.

With the exception of Cook's Corners, no one lives on the western section of the Great Windfall today. The old Wind-

ALBERT
FOWLER

fall road that once connected farms and hunting lodges is now closed to public use, its place taken by Route 3, the state highway two miles south, which passes through the village of Cranberry Lake and joins the old road east of the Grass River bridge. The western section of the Windfall is now a private game preserve, and the old road a deer runway.

Loyd Davis, long-time resident of Cranberry Lake, was concerned about the deer on the Windfall during the winter of 1960. While snows were deep, the deer had killed many of the young pine planted by the State Conservation Department, and Loyd had found several yearlings dead of starvation. He spoke persuasively of the need for a snowmobile to bring in feed in other such hard winters.

But winters of the mid-sixties have been mild. Deer on and near the Windfall are as abundant as they were a century ago, a fact well known to hunters. In recent years a thriving trailer camp has grown up in the clearing around Cook's Corners. Most of the owners are seasonal residents, members of a fish and game club. But there are a few year-round folk too, including the Thomases, descendants of early settlers of both Cranberry Lake and the Windfall. All of these people, newcomers and old-timers alike, and other people for miles around, speak familiarly of the Windfall of 1845 as part of the pattern of their lives. Its roots go deep in the folk memory of the Cranberry Lake region.

CHAPTER III

Bill Rasbeck's Diary

ATWOOD MANLEY

CRANBERRY LAKE was still a hunter's and fisherman's paradise when the first of Bill Rasbeck's entries were set down in diary form in 1887. The lake had undergone great changes, however, since Bowles and his companions poled up the Oswegatchie. A dam built in 1865–67 at the outlet had raised the water level and ringed the shores with drowned timber; it had also formed the nucleus of a small settlement. Hugh McConnell, who had helped build the dam, became its first tender. In 1871 Dick Thomas built a log inn nearby. William R. Bishop later bought the inn and operated it as Bishop's Hotel, long a favorite rendezvous of sportsmen. Thomas stayed on as guide. The growing demand for guides attracted other settlers, such as Bill Rasbeck. Yet the settlement grew slowly. What is now the village of Cranberry Lake had fewer than fifteen buildings in 1900.

By 1864 a new road had been cut from the Lake George Road southward to the Windfall. It was soon after extended to the lake and gave Cranberry a link with thriving villages in the northern part of St. Lawrence County. Citizens of Canton, the county seat, were now within a day's drive by buckboard. For them the great South Woods, as the Adirondacks were called in the northern tier of counties, came to mean Cranberry Lake.

As farms were established along the Windfall, a road was extended eastward from Cook's Corners to Sevey's. Connections on the west were slow to come. In 1889 the Carthage and Adirondack Railway reached Oswegatchie Station and Benson Mines. From the former place, a poor road of seven miles led to the Inlet, whence a boat could be taken to the foot of the lake. From the latter, a road cut early in the 1890's to Newton Falls and Cook's Corners gave Cranberry its first direct link on the west.

Bill Rasbeck was one of three brothers who spent their lives in the woods and made Cranberry their home. He was well known as a guide and much sought after by those who came to Bishop's Hotel. The famous Rasbeck Hole up Dead Creek Flow bears his name and commemorates his skill as an angler. His diary, which extends over a period of thirty years, constitutes an unusually intimate record of the life of that time, set down in brief, crisp sentences by a busy man at the end of a busy day. The pocket volumes, one for each year, were handed down to his nephew Floyd Rasbeck and are now in the Adirondack collection of the St. Lawrence University library.

The diary was first excerpted for the readers of Canton's *St. Lawrence Plaindealer* in the 1930's by Williston Manley. Now his son, Atwood Manley, has gone back to the diary to make a selection and arrangement of entries with emphasis on the historical setting. His commentary is drawn from a lifelong acquaintance with Cranberry Lake and its people.

There were three Rasbeck brothers, William, Harrison, and George, best known at Cranberry Lake as Bill, Has, and Gib. Their folks lived down on Porter Hill in a corner of the town of Hermon, not far from Trout Lake and about twenty-five miles from Cranberry. Bill was born in 1840, Has in 1843, and Gib much later in 1853.

After exploring the woods of the Grass River valley above the Clifton iron mines, Bill Rasbeck built a hunting camp a few miles south of the hamlet of Clarksboro, which was settled after the opening of the mines in 1866 and is today abandoned. The camp was enclosed and fit for winter use. As time went on, Bill began shuttling back and forth between his camp and Cranberry Lake, with Has as companion. Later Gib joined them, and finally Gib's boy, Floyd.

Bill was an unusual guide and hunter in that he found time to keep a diary pretty regularly till close to the time of his death in 1917. It is uncertain when he first came to Cranberry Lake. Floyd thought it was in the early 1870's. Canton's *St. Lawrence Plaindealer* carried an item in 1882 reporting that Asa Daily had been to the lake fishing with Bill Rasbeck as his guide.

The first entry in Bill's diary is dated Wednesday, February 23, 1887, when Bill was wintering with the family at Porter Hill:

"Weather verry clear & pleasant. I stayed at M. Guthries. Choped a little wood in the forenoon & then went down to the village. A. G. Wooley came back with me & stayed all night.

Bill Rasbeck's Diary

"February 24: Rainy in the forenoon & snowed terably till after dark. I left Mr. Guthries at 8 A.M. for camp on Grass R. with Arth Kinney. Kinny [*sic*] went for Gene Smiths camp things. We got to camp at 12, got dinner, took a good drink of whisky, got dinn, done up the camp work, packed up Smiths things & then Arthur went or started for home. He stayed to Clifton all night. I stayed at camp.

"February 25: Quite cold but clear. I went out gumming this afternoon. I got 1½ [lbs.] of gum. When I came in found Willard Howland & Dan Town at camp. They stayed all night.

"February 26: Terable winday but not very cold. I stayed in camp & cooked to prepare for a trip to the Carncross camp gumming. Howland & Town started this morning for the Carncross camp. They went there but came back & stayed all night with me.

"February 27: A terible wind & snow storm. Willard, Dan & myself started this morning for the Carncross camp. Went by road to Tooley Pond & then took the lumber road to the R then folowed up the River to camp. Dan went through the ice. He got one leg wet to the middle. We got to camp about noon. We thawed & choped ice & shoveled snow & split shingles or shakes to cover camp with. Put in a bed & got supper etc.

"February 28: Clear and cold. We three started out gumming this morning. We went north about one mile to the woolf hole then northwest about one half mile to Spruce Pond then N.W. a gumming. I only got 2¼ lbs. I got in camp at 3 o clock. The Boys did not get much gum. They caught two fawns, patted & played with them a while & then let them go. They got in camp about 4 o clock."

The following day the three "boys" got twenty-five pounds

Bill Rasbeck

Rasbeck and his brothers Has and Gib were popular guides in the heyday of Bishop's Hotel. Has was Frederic Remington's favorite guide, and at one time he and Bill ran camps for fishermen and hunters at Brandy Brook and Stony Point, near Sucker Brook, and at Darning Needle Pond. (Courtesy Atwood Manley)

Bishop's Hotel in the 1890's

"Guests . . . expected 'mountain goat' or 'lamb' by the heaping platter." (Photo by Irving D. Vann)

of spruce gum. "Willard & I caught a deer, an old doe. We looked it over till we were satisfied & then let her go. She was as we thought quite fat." The gumming lasted until March 4, when Willard and Dan went home. Bill stayed in his camp on the Grass River.

Gumming furnished more than pin money for Bill and his friends, but it was a part-time occupation. With a gunny sack slung from the shoulder or a packbasket on the back, they would take off for the dark timber. The resin from spruce trees often accumulated on the bark, some in rough masses, some in big blisters, often well up where limbs and branches forked out. To remove these batches of gum, they used a hatchet if the gum was within reach, but more often they used a "gummer." This was a homemade affair, usually a hickory or ash pole six to eight feet long. At the upper end it had a combination cutter and basket. The cutter had a knifelike square edge, and the chunk of gum usually fell into the basket, which hung directly below the cutter. Bill would pass from tree to tree as he located spruce gum. When the basket was nearly full and getting heavy, he would lower the pole and transfer the gum to his gunny sack or packbasket.

Much of the gum Bill and his friends marketed went to Rowe's Spruce Gum Factory in Russell, operated by two brothers, Mike and Jack Rowe. This brand became so firmly established that today one can still purchase it in some St. Lawrence River towns, such as Brockville, Ontario. Mike Rowe did not supply the only market for Bill Rasbeck's gumming. The diary shows that Bill often sold both blister and resin gum to George Burt, who ran the village store in Russell and who in turn sold it to one factory or another.

The blister gum which had hardened on the tree was as pure gum as could be found, and the factory had only to break it into small chunks and bag and label it. The resin gum was rather soft and sticky and was mixed with bits of bark, moss, lichens, and insects. This resin went into the kettles, was boiled to the consistency of syrup, skimmed and strained, and then poured into molds to harden. It was wrapped in wax paper, boxed, and sold to stores throughout northern New York, across the river in Canada, and even in cities like Boston.

"March 24: George Guthrie and I started for camp on Grass River this morning at 10 o clock. Reached camp about 3 in the afternoon. We got supper & eat nearly a peck of potatoes and a loaf of bread. Its now about dark. We will spend the evening in reading & singing & perhaps have a prayer or two."

Bill Rasbeck was more than a nominal Christian. Later he worked on the new church at Cranberry Lake, helped Sam Bancroft install the organ, and was on hand to listen to "the new minister."

"March 26: George & I went over East near Slouch Pond a-gumming. Geo got 3½ lbs of gum & I got 4¾. . . . After dinner we cut wood & I filed the saw. Set mouse traps. We caught one."

While at the Grass River camp George and Bill harvested three to five pounds of gum a day. They also "gathered balsam," probably for camp beds. They returned home on April 2, and during the next few days Bill whittled gum to prepare it for market. He sold it in Russell at eighty cents a pound. Guiding paid better at three dollars a day and food, but gumming was not bad for off-season work.

"April 2: George Guthrie & I pledged ourselves this morning to not either of us drink whisky till the 4th of July next."

Beer was another thing. On April 15 Bill was back at the river camp brewing wintergreen and elderberry beer. On April 15 the snow was "2 feet deep" in the woods, "too deep for gumming." Bill spent a few days about camp.

"April 18: I started from camp this morning for Cranberry Lake. I got there at 2 o clock & went over to Ab Thompsons. I stayed at Mr. Bishops over night. . . .

"April 19: I called at George Sawyers a few minutes this morning & then started for camp but stoped & took dinner with Sam Bancroft."

Bill spent the latter part of April and the first week in

May at Porter Hill, doing chores. On May 8 he wrote, "The River drivers were sweeping the pond of logs." On the ninth he "made a keg of [wintergreen] beer." On the eleventh he was back in camp and immediately began gumming, with fair results. The weather was warmer, and the trout were beginning to bite. On May 15 he wrote, "This afternoon I went a-fishing and I got 7 trout."

With Will Gordon and Donald Stewart he set out on May 26 for Cranberry Lake and spent the night at Bishop's.

"May 27: We started for Grass pond about 5 o clock this morning. Got there about ten. Caught a few trout for dinner. This afternoon we caught about 54 trout & had lots of fun." The Grass Pond he refers to lies three or four miles south of the head of the lake.

On May 28 they caught "59 trout & lots of bullhead." They were back at the hotel by dark.

"June 2: I helped Mr. Bishop log today. Mr. Dean & Mr. Madeson came here today from Gouverneur. Mr. M. Kane & Mr. O. M. Baker also came this afternoon."

By this and succeeding entries it becomes evident that Bill had changed his abode. He had moved from his river camp and now stayed at the lake. For several years he occupied a shack or shed at the rear and to one side of Bishop's Hotel. He helped Riley Bishop at odd jobs, putting in a dock, shoring up timbers under the hotel, hoeing potatoes. He was also in a preferred position whenever guests arrived at the hotel and needed a guide.

His diary records his proficiency with a gun in floating and in jacking deer by frequent mention of his taking a "hog" or "beef" or just "a ——." Sometimes he boldly named it a deer, buck, or doe. The hotel table had to be supplied with meat in and out of season, and this sort of "hog" business loomed large in the Adirondack economy of those days. Guests at Bishop's expected "mountain goat" or "lamb" by the heaping platter. Parties did not come to Cranberry principally for rest and fresh air. They usually came to catch trout and kill

Chan Westcott

Westcott was a hunter, guide, and early settler. His widow, Glencora Westcott, now approaching her 100th birthday, has long been a source of much early history and legend. (Photo by Irving D. Vann)

deer. Every camp worth the name had a tub of trout in the spring and a saddle of venison hanging somewhere in the brush.

But the surest and readiest means for making money was the city market. Shipping venison was an accepted way of earning a living. As summer turned into fall and the leaves took on their painted hues, the meat business brisked up. Saddles of venison frequently left the lake by the wagon load, destined for the nearest railroad station. From there they were expressed to the cities until the law against such sales was properly enforced, and even then the business was carried on locally through the village market. Berkley's lumber camp near the dam became the general clearing house for shipments of meat.

Bill Rasbeck's Diary

Gib Rasbeck, according to local tradition, took out the last full load of saddles from the lake in 1890. It was about then that New York State began to enforce the game law of 1879, which, as amended over the next ten years, narrowly limited the sale and transportation of venison. Under cover of darkness Gib set out from Berkley's for Porter Hill with a full load of frozen saddles. He made the family barn before sunup. The following night he drove through to Madrid Springs. The New York Central agent in Canton rejected the shipment of venison, but the agent of the Rutland Railroad accepted it. So Gib sent that last load to the Boston market by the Rutland.

"June 3: We went up to the head of the lake to blow out the bog. We cut & blowed off a piece & drawed it out." The lake was not yet cleared of floating bogs, which occasionally got in the way of boats and had to be broken up and removed.

The "wether" was fair on June 6, and Bill gathered wintergreen roots for beer in the morning and worked for Ab Thompson logging and planting potatoes in the afternoon.

"June 7: I made beer. This afternoon I helped Mr. Bishop get out dock timber. This evening I went with Ab Thompson, Sam Bancroft & Mr. Mullen over to Sucker brook fishing suckers. We got about 150 lbs."

Cranberry was noted for more than trout. Irving Bacheller in *Coming Up the Road* tells how as a lad in the early 1870's he went to the head of Cranberry Lake "a-suckering" while the run was on at the mouth of Sucker Brook.

After dinner on June 8 Bill "worked for Mr. Bishop building a privy."

"June 16: Mr. Howlet & party came here tonight to stay till the 30th." [A. A. Howlett and Albert H. Hiscock of Syracuse had built Tramps Retreat in 1886.] Apparently the fishing was poor, and this party broke camp on June 26. From then on into July there was little activity. The fishing was mediocre and the hunting poor.

"July 7: I went over to Olmstead Pond hunting & stayed all night. I killed a hedgehog."

Bill was not only a woodsman and guide but something of a professional cook, who hired out to cook for lumbermen on the spring log drives. This explains why in the front of his 1887 diary he pasted recipes for brown bread, baked beans, Johnny cake, rice pudding, berry pie, cream of tartar biscuits, oatmeal, "Warner's Safe Yeast," and so on. It may also explain why so many of the hotel guests preferred Bill as a guide, and why he and his brother Has often teamed up in guiding parties around the lake. Has was the more dedicated hunter, trapper, and fisherman of the two.

"July 10: I stayed at the hotel all day. Not much going on. Billie Simpson & Mr. Wallace returned from their fishing trip. Earl & Lord went to Brandy Brook fishing. They caught about 15 or 20 lbs." "Earl" was Earl Knox, born in Russell in St. Lawrence County and living in New York City, on his annual trip to the lake with Chester Lord, editor of the old New York *Sun*.

"July 12: I comenced work for Mr. Taner [*sic*] & Mr. Mc-Clair this morning. We went into camp at Brandy brook."

From then until July 20 Bill was on the move. Bill, Wallace, and Simpson found Chan Westcott and Ab Thompson hunting at Curtis Pond. "Floated awhile in the evening but didn't see anything." On July 14 Bill "started for our camp on

brandy brook with a jagg of meat which Mr. Wallace got."
Two days later the party went raspberrying. Mr. Tanner fell
and spilled his berries while getting into the boat, but there
were enough left for berries and biscuits with supper.

On July 20 they went "a-frogging" on Bear Mountain
Pond. "Only got 2 frogs and saw 2 deer." After supper "we
went back again frogging but shot 4 & blowed them all to bits
& couldn't find them."

"July 22: We three went to the head of the Plains on the big
inlet. We stayed all night at S. H. Ward's camp."

This was "Uncle Steve" Ward, well known at Cranberry
Lake through several generations. Born February 4, 1837, near
Lake Bonaparte, he made his first trip to Cranberry with his
father when he was seven. He joined the Union Army in the
Civil War and came back with a slug in his leg. He was lame
ever after, and in his last years his bad leg kept him from getting around much in the woods. He died in August, 1928, at the
age of ninety-one.

"July 27: We three [Tanner, McClair, and Bill] went up
Brandy brook fishing this morning. I left them about Eleven
o clock & went a hunting. Got a beef."

"August 1: Verry warm. We fished a little this morning &
then Mr. Taner & I went gull hunting. We got two gulls &
this afternoon we broke camp & packed up & loaded our
stuff on the steamer & went down to Bishops."

For most of August, Bill guided for a Mr. Holmes and for
Judge Smith and family. Luck in hunting was poor. On Sep-
tember 2 Bill went to Witch Bay with Willard, Nelt, and
Fred Howland to hunt. "Did not get a thing but a wet jacket."

After two weeks "down home" Bill was back "with the
party from Russell." Hunting picked up. From Brandy Brook
they moved to Bassout Pond. "Set up our tent & fixed up in
good shape. . . . We got a doe." Two days later they went to Cat
Mountain Pond, "caught all we wanted to eat," and "killed a
buck." The next night at Glasby Pond John Stewart "killed
one & wounded another." The following day Charles Smith
and Art Kinney killed a deer to make four in six days.

Uncle Steve Ward
(*standing*)
and Cornelius Carter
(Adirondack Poet)

Uncle Steve, a Civil War veteran, had a camp on the Indian Mountain shore and was a storehouse of Cranberry history in his old age. "Old Man" Carter had a camp at Carter's Landing, not far downriver from High Falls on the upper Oswegatchie. His name is also associated with Carter's Springhole nearby, one of the best places for large trout—3-, 4-, and 5-pounders. (Courtesy Atwood Manley)

The Rasbeck Brothers (*Bill at the oars*)

"Bill and Has went hunting . . ." Note the "hop poles" in the background. (Courtesy Atwood Manley)

46

Bill Rasbeck's Cottage, Cranberry Lake Village

"Tonight (November 2, 1888), I am in my cottage for the first time." (Courtesy Atwood Manley)

Bill Rasbeck and Party at His Camp on Stony Point

"Hardly did one party leave . . . before another arrived and hired Bill." (Courtesy Atwood Manley)

On October 3 Bill, Has, and a man named Harrison "moved camp to Witch bay on the lake. After dinner we went over to East bay & to a pond. We saw a bear up a tree. As he dropped off the tree we shot at it & we think we got one bullet in it but lost it. We found the Hermon party in camp when we came back."

On October 4 Bill killed a deer and the next day a buck.

Late in October Bill and Has went back to their old Grass River camp. Bill, lame with rheumatism, left camp two days later for home, where he made a pair of moccasins, brewed yeast, and sponged bread.

On November 13 Bill was back in camp with Has, Barney Burns, and J. Snell. The next day Has and Bill each got a deer near South Brook, and Bill got another two days later.

Trapping then became the order of the day. Bill set his traps and on November 22 caught a "saple . . . not six rods from camp." He got another a few days later.

The "saple" Bill often trapped was the sable, of the marten genus. He also mentions taking an occasional fisher. According to a copy of Belt, Butler Company's price list of 1911 attached to one of the diaries, a fisher pelt brought from one to sixteen dollars depending on its condition, and a dark marten skin might fetch as much as $15.50.

The year 1888 did not get under way at the lake for Bill until spring.

"May 6: Ed Franklin, Ab Thompson [both year-round residents] & I went to Cat Mountain Pond fishing. We got here about night, cut wood & fixed up for night. The ice went out of Cranberry Lake this afternoon.

"May 7: We fished & I looked for Ab's boat. We did not find the boat. . . . Franklin caught 40 trout. This afternoon we all fished. We got about 25 or 30 lbs. . . .

"May 9: We came home with 30 lbs. trout. After dinner I shaved shingles & painted my boat. My trout came to 2.00 dollars."

On May 10 Bill began guiding for Fred Howlett and Bert

Hiscock, probably at Tramps Retreat. Three days later "Fred & Sawyer [George, the guide] went to Curtis pond fishing. They caught 15 weighing 17 lbs."

Bill purchased a lot on the lake shore about a hundred yards from Bishop's Hotel and prepared to build a cottage. Apparently he paid a hundred dollars for the lot over a period of two years. On May 15 doors and windows came, but the cottage had to wait. Ab Thompson and Bill went to Darning Needle Pond, built a camp, and enjoyed good fishing.

Bill Rasbeck's Diary

"May 21: We sold 14¾ lbs. of trout at 20¢ a lb. Salted up an old deer lick."

On May 26 Ab and Bill began guiding Senator Dolph Lynde and Worth Chamberlain from Canton at "Darkneedle" Pond. "We got a fine lot of trout." On May 30 Bill was off for Russell to attend "Dekoration."

"June 1: I went with Ab Thompson to build a camp on brandy brook for a winter camp." This was an enclosed camp up the creek from Brandy Brook Flow. It had gabled ends and a bark floor. Bill made many trips there for fishing, hunting, and trapping.

"July 10: Fred Howlet caught a big trout today, weight 5 lbs. 14 oz. Chet Lord got a big catch."

Howlett's big trout was a record for years. Another monster trout is credited to John R. Mills, gatekeeper of the dam. It is said to have tipped the scales at five pounds, twelve ounces.

From July 20 to August 1, 1888, Bill was busy with a big party from Syracuse. Two different trips were made to the top of Graves Mountain. Sixteen guests and two guides went along. "We got back to Bishops about one terable hungry."

Hardly did one party leave that summer before another arrived and hired Bill. The Ives and Washburn party came in, and Bill "floated" Ives on Bear Mountain Pond. "Got 2 shots & got one deer. I received 5 dollars as a present for my good paddling." Luck was not always good. Many days the trout refused to bite, and time after time hunting left the men empty handed.

A lull in late September gave Bill and his friends a chance to work on the new cottage. Ab shingled the house, and others put up the cornicing. Holes were cut for setting windows, a piazza was begun, and on October 19 Bill commenced his stable.

November 2 was a red-letter day in Bill's life. "I moved this afternoon. Tonight I am in my cotage for the first time." By way of a salute two flocks of Canada geese flew over. On November 17 "Ab & I went to Brandy Brook. We each got a hog." Bill and Ab did some trapping that fall and also some gumming. Bill got a total of sixty-five pounds of rough spruce gum, and Ab got forty-one pounds.

Hunting, fishing, trapping, gumming, and guiding—this combination fashioned the way of life at the lake in the 1880's. To these five occupations would soon be added a sixth—lumbering. In the next decade also, "civilization" moved in, with fine summer residences, inns and hotels, naphtha and steam launches, leg-of-mutton sleeves, bustles, and pompadours. Like others, Bill adjusted, gradually to be sure, cautiously, always with a weather eye on the big Lone Pine to see which way the wind was blowing.

That a change was coming became evident in 1889, the spring when Bill signed up to cook for the spring drive of the Canton Lumber Company. "I had to cook all day," reads the entry of April 15. "We fed over 40 men today in all, some coming and some going out." The number soon grew to fifty. For ten years Bill cooked for the company during the spring drive, which lasted two or three weeks, just long enough to get the winter cut on its way down the Grass to the mills in Canton. Bill wrote of the log jams at Rainbow Falls and of the "frenchmen" that broke them up. That year the camp was down Clarksboro way. Logging had not yet reached Cranberry, but it was soon to come. King Lumber and the summer crowd put a new zip into the lake's economy. The steamer *Howlett* was succeeded by the *Lakeview*. Then came other passenger-mail boats like the *Helen* and the *Wanakena,* delivering mail and freight to camps and hotels and running excursions. Bill's diaries clocked off these changes impassively.

His own life changed little from year to year. But he was content with his time and place. The diary never speaks of wishes or regrets, of past or future; only of the day's activities and the weather. The seasonal rounds of a woodsman's life and the variable Adirondack weather seemed to satisfy fully Bill's need of change. The weather fascinated him. He never failed to note it.

Bill Rasbeck's Diary

"I went up dead creek to hunt," Bill wrote on July 14, 1892. "After I got there Judge Van & Earl [Knox] came up there & also the game constable. So I came back to flat rock bay and got one." Constable or no constable.

In that year of 1892, when Bill turned fifty-two, signs of both age and renewal appeared in the diary. "I went to Canton on the stage to get my teeth," he wrote on May 25. Yet Bill still had plenty of gimp. Autumn brought an Indian summer romance. Cranberry had not only a church but also a school by now. Among the older "scholars" were two sisters, usually escorted by their brother, Donald Compton. On October 11 Bill noted that "two of the young ladies and Mr. Compton" had just called on him; a week later, "two of the school girls called to see me tonight." The sisters called again on October 28, and the next day "Miss Compton rode with [me] in boat to Sams [Sam Bancroft, keeper of the dam] and back." That afternoon Bill "moped and cleaned up" his cottage, the next day he patched his pants, and on the evening of October 31 "the two Misss Compton & brother were here. We played a game called Tidle-de wink." For the first two weeks in November meetings were almost daily. Bill rowed the two sisters back and forth along the lake front—to school, to Bishop's Hotel, and to Sam Bancroft's place, where they were apparently rooming. Bill's preference for the older sister, Iva, soon began to ripen. "Ive asked me to come down after them," he noted with satisfaction on November 4. Two days later he rowed the sisters to Sam's place, and that evening they called on him in company with their brother. On November 11, "Donald Compton and his two sisters were here this morning. I got the oldest one, Ive, in my lap & huged her up in good shape." Three days later Bill rowed "young Compton and Miss Failing down to Sams & fetched Miss Iva Compton back to my landing." Bill was not strong on sentiment. On November 17 he noted the end of the affair in his usual blunt way. The complete entry for that day reads: "Verry fine [the weather]. Has came up tonight. I rowed the two Misses Compton to school & 3 other scholars. Then young Compton & I went up to brandy brook to take up my bear traps. We got dinner & came back at 4 o clock. The 2 Compton girls were over here tonight & we sugared off. I went home with Iva Compton. Got the mitten."

One last visit from the brother and one of the sisters on November 22 followed this rejection of his suit, and then the Comptons pass out of the diary for good. Bill and Has went hunting almost every day the rest of that season.

Bill's diary faithfully records the changes of the next two decades—the coming of logging operations to the shores of the lake, the forest fire of 1903, the growing popularity of Cranberry as a summer resort. But in the new century Bill was no longer so active as he used to be. In 1910, the year he turned seventy, his diary noted, "I still sit in the house most of the time," and a few days later, "laid abed all day."

In 1912 Has, too, was in failing health and on August 24 "moved over to Gibs this afternoon to stay." That year was not a good one for the two elder brothers. No longer able to move about freely in the woods, Bill, known thus far as an easy-going, even-tempered man, now had testy spells. "This afternoon," he wrote on September 17, "I put the minister out in the road. As he was determined to come into my house I ordered him into the road. He would not go so I had to put him out of my yard." This act may not have brought on bad luck, but didn't help to avert it. Less than a month later, on October 12, Bill, after his usual comment on the weather, added abruptly: "My house burned to the ground tonight about 6 o clock. Only saved what stuff there was in the kitchen." (The diaries must have been with the stuff in the kitchen.) Bill moved into his woodshed. A week later he noted that he was very lame with rheumatism and was taking things easy.

Bill Rasbeck's Diary

Without the woods as a prompter, Bill had little to say now. Most of the entries for 1915 and 1916 simply record the weather, sometimes in a single word. Bill was still able to tend his garden occasionally, but could not do much else. On September 14, 1915, he wrote, "I am not doing much," and a week later, "I am having a rest now days." But on July 30, 1916, he noted, "I still work at my potatoes." A week later Charles and John Thompson took him to Oswegatchie "for a ride in their otto." All but three dated pages in the notebook for 1916 have entries, however brief, through August 7; then blank pages separate just two more jottings—for October 17 and December 10—in Bill's diary. The hand at the pencil remained steady, but the old woodsman had nothing more to report. Not even the weather.

Cranberry Lake

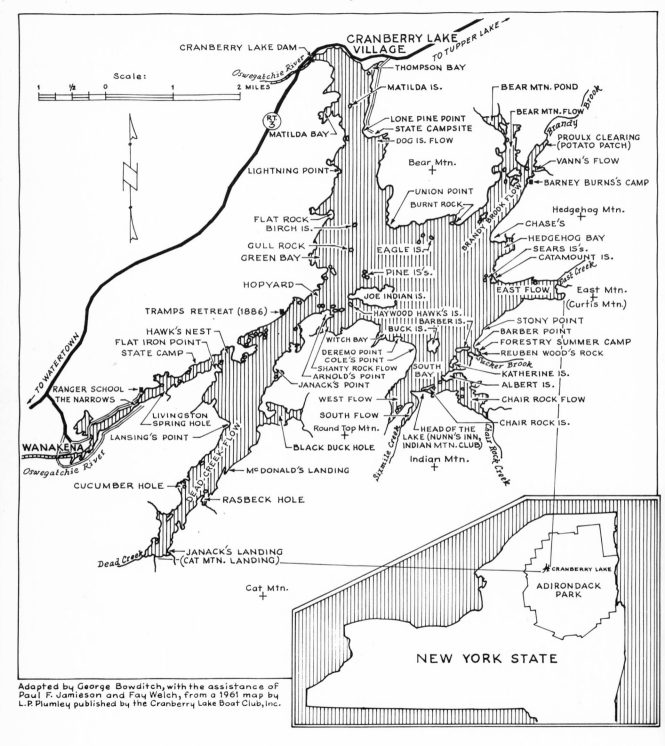

Scale:

Adapted by George Bowditch, with the assistance of
Paul F. Jamieson and Fay Welch, from a 1961 map by
L.P. Plumley published by the Cranberry Lake Boat Club, Inc.

NEW YORK STATE

ADIRONDACK PARK

CRANBERRY LAKE

CHAPTER IV

Reuben Wood, Great Fisherman

Irving G. Vann

CRANBERRY LAKE, its inlets, its outlet, and the outlying ponds were excellent trout waters, according to the rumor spread among sportsmen of the East in the 1870's and 1880's. In 1874 and again in 1880 Verplanck Colvin's published reports of his survey of the wilderness just south of Cranberry Lake told a dramatic story of the discovery of lost ponds and of two ponds where only one was supposed to be. Country such as this could not long be neglected by William H. H. Murray, clergyman-author whose *Adventures in the Wilderness* (1869) had drawn thousands of sportsmen, health-seekers, and tourists to the Adirondacks. In 1875 Murray visited Cranberry, camped at the head of Inlet Flow, fished in the rapids of the Inlet, and perhaps asked his guide to row him upstream into that wonderland of virgin trout waters Colvin had just described.

In 1876 *Forest and Stream* published the first of many articles on the fishing in Cranberry waters. After launching a Rushton "sporting boat" at Griffin's, the writer reached the lake, as Bowles had in 1852, by pushing up the Oswegatchie with three carries, past the "old Indian fishing grounds," and on two miles farther to the dam at the foot of the lake, where he joined friends. On their best day's fishing he and his companions caught seventy "fine trout" in a creek on the Windfall. Another party took ninety-eight trout on their first day's fishing in 1888 near Sternberg's on the Inlet.

In the same year *Forest and Stream* reported some record-breaking catches. The dam tender had caught below the dam a brook trout weighing five pounds, thirteen ounces, and on July 10, 1888, A. A. Howlett, of Syracuse, had taken on the Inlet one of five pounds, fourteen ounces, the largest brook trout recorded up to that time as caught by anglers in Adirondack waters. "The lake itself," boasted an ad for the Cranberry Lake House (Bishop's Hotel) in Wallace's *Guide* for 1887, "is thronged with trout and contains no other fish." This publicity was all too successful in bringing fishermen to Cranberry.

Reuben Wood, one of the early comers, came up from Syracuse to try his skill at Sucker Brook. In 1878 he spent a summer vacation there with his friends Irving G. Vann, lawyer and future mayor of Syracuse and author of the following sketch, and A. Judd Northrup, author of *Camps and Tramps in the Adirondacks* (1880).

Reub Wood's name is familiar to trout fishermen today who still use the fly which he invented. The name of his friend Seth Green is attached to another fly still in use. Wood was one of the people of international fame who came to Cranberry Lake. His reputation as a fly fisherman was already widespread in 1878, and five years later, in England, he won the international fly-casting contest, with the Prince of Wales as onlooker.

The lake was still a fine fishing ground in 1895 when Irving G. Vann had a memorial inscription to Reuben Wood cut into the face of a large boulder set in the solitudes the old angler was fond of at the mouth of Sucker Brook. But the end of an era was in sight. The ax had already been set to the tree. The virgin forest around Sucker Brook succumbed early in the new century. Then the summer camp of the State College of Forestry moved in and for the next fifty years surrounded the boulder with buildings and bustling activity. The lettering on the rock, lichened and hardly legible, was largely forgotten. But in 1966 the forestry camp moved away, and once again a respite of solitude congenial to old anglers settled down over Sucker Brook.

Reuben Wood was born at Greenbush, opposite Albany, in 1822 and died at Syracuse, February 16, 1884. His active life was devoted to the management of a sporting goods store in Syracuse, in which he carried a large and well-chosen stock of articles for hunters and fishermen, especially the latter. He was devoted to sport throughout his life and was apparently as fond of the gun as of the rod until he was nearly fifty years of age, when he laid aside his gun and afterward used his rod exclusively.

A genial, whole-souled man, simple hearted and natural, he was the friend of everyone who knew him. His beard was full, his hair long, and both were nearly white during the last ten years of his life. His appearance was venerable, but above

Reuben Wood, 1867

A "genial gentleman and great fisherman," Wood was fond of the solitudes of the Cranberry Lake of his day. (Courtesy Onondaga Historical Association)

all it was kindly. He had great skill in casting the fly, and long observation had given him knowledge of the habits of fish, which enabled him to tell with remarkable accuracy where they were and when they would bite. He invariably used the artificial fly and could cast it not only a long distance but with surprising delicacy and accuracy, so that the flies would sink with a gentle fluttering motion onto the water in close imitation of the natural fly.

He took the first prize for many years at all the fly-casting tournaments in this state, except on two occasions when he intentionally allowed Mr. Seth Green, his lifelong friend, to take the first prize by secretly casting his fly a little short, so that the second prize fell to him and the first to Mr. Green.

In 1883 he was appointed by Mr. Spencer F. Beard, the United States Commissioner, to take charge of the Angling Department of the American Exhibition at the International Fishers' Exposition in London. While there he made many friends and was invited on several occasions to fish in English waters. Although he had never fished with a dry fly such as English sportsmen use in nearly all of their streams, he distanced everyone who fished with him, or who had fished on the same stream that season, in the size of his catches. He participated in the casting tournaments and took first prize against the world for salmon casting and for single-handed trout casting. In contesting with two-handed trout rods, which were previously unknown to him, he took the second prize.

He taught many sportsmen to cast the fly. Many times he could have been seen on the bank of the Erie Canal in front of the courthouse at Syracuse giving practical instruction to young men, and sometimes to old men, in fly casting. His custom was at first to bind the right elbow of his pupil to his side so that he could not use the arm motion, as it is called, but was wholly dependent upon the wrist motion, which is the main secret of success in casting the fly.

All of these pupils were his devoted friends, and they revere his memory as that of a father. Some of them he took with him on excursions to the Adirondacks and elsewhere, and one of them in later years, moved by gratitude and affection, caused an inscription to his memory to be carved upon a rock at the mouth of Sucker Brook in Cranberry Lake. For a long time the rock had a large pine tree growing upon it, but a few years ago the pine was destroyed by fire. Mr. Wood used to clamber up on the rock, which is about fifteen feet high and nearly as many feet square at the base but somewhat narrower at the top, and, seated with his fishing friends about the roots of the tree and smoking a cigar, which he always had in his mouth during waking moments, he would tell delightful fishing stories and make suggestions for the sport of the following day.

It was his habit to carefully observe, about sundown, the color of the flies upon the water, and he would select his cast for the next morning so as to imitate the prevailing color of the night before.

The rock is known on the maps of St. Lawrence County as Reuben Wood Rock, and upon it is the following inscription carved in enduring letters: "In memory of Reuben Wood, a genial gentleman and great fisherman who was fond of these solitudes."

Alas, the sound of the ax is now heard and the operations of lumberman are now seen about his favorite camping spots on Cranberry Lake, and the solitudes he loved so well are not so dense as when he was accustomed to visit the woods or even as they were in 1895 when the inscription was cut. The woods may fade away under the devastating hand of the lumberman, the trout may diminish or disappear, but the memory of Reuben Wood will last as long in the minds of his surviving friends as anything that with their last consciousness they are able to recall.

The Reuben Wood Rock

Located at the mouth of Sucker Brook Flow, the rock was inscribed to Wood's memory by his friend Irving G. Vann. This picture was taken in the 1930's when the Forestry Camp boathouses had replaced the surrounding solitudes. (Photo by David Lane)

CHAPTER V

Frederic Remington

ATWOOD MANLEY

ATWOOD MANLEY knows more about Frederic Remington's northern New York background and love for the Adirondacks, centering in Cranberry Lake, than anyone else. Like Remington, he was born and brought up in Canton and knew members of the Remington family and their friends. He is the author of a booklet, *Frederic Remington in the Land of His Youth,* which was published in 1961 in connection with the centennial observance of the artist's birth.

The present sketch concerns Remington's vacations on Cranberry Lake and canoe trip down the Oswegatchie River and portrays him as sportsman and lover of the woods.

"Remington is on the way in."

From 1889 to 1899 this message was almost perennial. Sometime during the summer or fall word would come up the line from Canton to Clifton to Cranberry Lake that Fred Remington was on the way. At the foot of the lake this was always welcome news.

From her kitchen at the log hotel Eliza Jane Bishop ("Auntie B.") would keep a watchful eye on Sam Bancroft's place near the state dam. The second she saw Fred's rig kicking up dust as it emerged from the forest, she would call to her niece, Nina Bishop, and the other waitresses in the dining room:

"Get on a hustle. Here he comes."

"So we'd hustle," recalled Nina Bishop Loucks many years later. "We'd put the two stoutest plank-bottom chairs just as close together before his place as we could get them. Remington's big bottom would fill them both, and how that man would eat. My, how he would eat!"

Word that Remington had arrived would spread like magic from one end of the lake to the other, around Lone Pine Point into Brandy Brook Flow, across to Judge Vann's place on Buck Island, over to Nunn's Inn at the head of the lake, from there to Fred Howlett's Tramps Retreat on Inlet Flow and up through the Hawk's Nest as far as Sternberg's. The news traveled like a fresh breeze blowing across the lake. Soon the guides would begin drifting down to the foot of the lake to bend a friendly elbow at Bishop's bar. Even the loons would set up a clatter. They seemed to sense that the crack from Remington's Winchester would soon be putting them through their fanciest diving tricks.

When Williston Manley and Everett Caldwell arrived at Bishop's one summer afternoon on their first trip to the lake, they found Fred Remington comfortably settled on the porch, easel and drawing pad before him, a rifle nearby ready for use when a loon hove in sight out on the lake, and a quart within easy reach.

"Remington was sketching," Williston Manley recounted. "He'd do that by the hour. No sooner would he finish something than he would tear the page from his drawing book, throw it on the floor, and start all over again on something else —a guide, a woods scene, a bird, a deer, whatever met his fancy. Mark [Williston's brother] once gathered up a whole sheaf of those loose pages from the floor and brought them home to Canton. They were lying around the house a long time. Nobody remembers what became of them."

Cranberry Lake became Remington's chosen Adirondack retreat long before those almost annual pilgrimages during the busy decade which marked his rise to fame as an artist of the Old West. He began going to the lake as a boy. It was remote then, a twelve-hour drive by team upcountry over rutty, rocky, backwoods roads. Cranberry was his initiation to the kind of life he glorified in his art—roughing it. There he became expert with the rifle, the split bamboo, and the paddle. He was as much at home in the stern seat of a canoe as in a Western saddle and loved it equally well.

While at Cranberry he could usually be found either at the head of the lake in a little camp on Witch Bay or at the foot in Bishop's log hotel. The original log section housed the bar in Remington's day, and overhead were the guides' quarters, reached by a ladder from the barroom. Attached to the log part of the hotel was the plain, rough-planked dining room and kitchen ell, the domain over which Auntie B. presided with authority. Such heaping helpings of salt pork and milk gravy, Fred's favorite dish, as this warm-hearted woman served up; such platters-full of crisply browned trout and succulent venison tenderloins and stews, with all the trimmings!

As a child Frederic Remington was exposed to tales of the fabulous trout fishing at Cranberry Lake and of the limitless deer feeding along its shore lines waiting for the hunter. The village of Canton, where he was born on October 4, 1861, where he spent the first eleven or twelve years of his life, and to which he was always returning, was a hotbed of Cranberry Lake addicts. Packard, the drygoods man; his crony Ellsworth, the shoe man; and J. Henry Rushton, Canton's world-famous canoe builder, made it to the lake regularly, as soon as word came down that the ice had gone out, that the maples were in bud, and the big speckles were rising to the fly. Ellsworth raised the first sail to adorn Cranberry's waters. He was next-door neighbor to Fred's grandfather, Deacon Sackrider. In 1862 J. B. Ellsworth and his lifelong companion, Packard, first packed in to the head of the lake over a blazed trail. They were the vanguard of a long and growing line of Cranberry enthusiasts to come from Canton.

No records can now be found to date precisely the time Fred Remington first stood on the beach in front of Bishop's, but it was in 1877, when he was sixteen, that the Canton *Plaindealer* announced, "Fred Remington, son of Col. S. P. Remington, is in town preparing for a trip into the woods." In

Frederic Remington

Riley Bishop and His Wife, Eliza Jane (Auntie B.)

A moment of peace on the porch of their hotel, usually the scene of bustling activity on Frederic Remington's arrival. (Courtesy Mrs. Albert Loucks)

Canton at that time a trip into the woods usually meant Cranberry.

In 1882 Remington was back in Canton from his position in Albany, where he was a member of Governor Alonzo Cornell's clerical staff, to prepare for a "summer vacation in the woods."

Remington's favorite uncle, Mart Remington, was at Cranberry in the summer of 1884 attempting to fight off the consumption he had contracted the year before while visiting Fred on his sheep ranch in Butler County, Kansas. Mart, who was living in a tiny log camp on the shore of Silver Lake just a stone's throw from Bishop's back door, drove down to Canton at great expense of strength to see Fred, who was back from the West and on his way to marry Eva Caten, the Gloversville beauty.

Among the Cranberry guides whom Remington knew were Chan Westcott; the three Rasbeck brothers, Has, Bill, and

Gib; the Thomas and the Thompson brothers, especially Ab Thompson, Cranberry's jack-of-all-trades; Barney Burns, whose Brandy Brook camp was the envy of all; and George Sawyer. They were a rough-hewn lot, the first of that breed Remington rubbed shoulders with long before he saw the plains west of the Mississippi. Bill Rasbeck's diaries, along with the *Plaindealer* files and the recollections of a few old-timers, make it possible to outline a picture of Frederic Remington's days at Cranberry Lake.

Frederic Remington

Has Rasbeck, who became Remington's favorite guide at Cranberry, once remarked: "Remington certainly got around a powerful lot, and he never stayed put for long anywhere."

During his professional career the artist was restless and unpredictable. Probably he owed most in the way of discipline to his wife Eva, or "Missie," as she was called. She tamed him as much as any living mortal could, cajoled and coaxed him into keeping at his art work. But he could never hold himself down to work in his New Rochelle studio for longer than two or three months at a stretch. Then he would pack up and take off, often for the West, sometimes for Europe, occasionally for the South during turkey-hunting season, or Mexico, or far back into the wilds of Canada.

But from 1889 to 1899 there was scarcely a summer when he did not turn up in Canton, and from there he would strike out for Cranberry by team. At the lake he could loaf as he pleased, but he also turned out a considerable portfolio of pictures where the great horned owl looked down on his campfire at night or the buck went whistling and crashing through the brush.

The year 1889 was one of the most notable in Remington's life. The articles on ranch life in the West which he had illustrated for Theodore Roosevelt, and which had been running in the *Century,* had made a hit with the public. In June of 1889 word came that Remington had won a silver medal in the international art exhibit in Paris. In the same year the publishing firm of Houghton Mifflin commissioned Remington to do a large number of illustrations for a deluxe edition of Long-

Hunter's Cabin in the Adirondacks, by Frederic Remington

The oil on panel (18¼″ x 28⅛″, date uncertain—between 1889 and 1897) is presently owned by the Adirondack Museum. The real subject of the painting (*see photo opposite*) was discovered during the preparation of this book. (Photo by Kennedy Galleries, Inc.)

fellow's *The Song of Hiawatha*. He had suddenly become famous. But he could not stay put anywhere for long.

He headed north to Canton, Missie with him of course. He converted his uncle Horace Sackrider's barn on State Street into a studio. "Mr. Remington can be found there almost any morning surrounded by attendants and horses," the *Plaindealer* reported. Evenings he and Missie would take a stroll about the village. For Remington a stroll was a constitutional, and he would go striding along ten paces ahead of his diminutive wife.

That was the June when Senator Dolph Lynde proposed

Ab Thompson's Cabin on Silver Pond,* about 1897

Built in Cranberry Lake Village, in 1884, this cabin was occupied by Ab and his wife (a Cook of Cook's Corners) and children until 1898, when the family moved into a new frame house nearby. George Thompson, present owner of the property and the fourth of Ab's six children, lived in the cabin until his sixth year. (Photo by Florence Vann Fowler) *Editor's note: Through an error on a USGS map, Silver Pond is also called Silver Lake.

a camping trip to Cranberry, the party to consist of his family, the Remingtons, and the family of John C. Keeler, the Canton attorney. Lynde and Keeler were then making heavy investments in Cranberry Lake timberlands. The eight who finally joined the party were Fred and Eva Remington, John and Mattie Keeler and their son John, and the three members of the Lynde family, the Senator, his wife Esther, and their daughter Grace, who had just finished her junior year in high school. This group of lively companions set out in two three-seated surreys. Their food and other supplies followed in a wagon.

Fred Remington took not only his rifle and rod but a goodly supply of canvases, drawing paper, oils, water colors, and other art materials, for he was already deep into the *Hiawatha* order, which required twenty-two full-scale paintings for page plates and three hundred and seventy-nine sketches and drawings, the largest single order he ever undertook.

Bill Rasbeck's diaries of 1889 give a daily record of that camping expedition:

Saturday, July 6: Has & I comenced to work for Keeler & Remington. We built camp all day. Built at or back of Wich Bay.

July 7: We worked verry hard, all building camp. I came down tonight to the house. Got 2 dozzen eggs of Murray Bancroft & 7 lbs nails of W R Bishop for Keeler & co.

July 8: We worked about camp till night. Then Mr. Remington & I went to bear mountain pond hunting. Did not see anything.

July 9: Has and I went to Darnkneedle Pond tonight. We got a ——— [Bill's way of covering up an infraction of the game laws]. It rained tonight till about 11 o'clock. Has & Keeler fished to brandy brook. Got 7 trout.

Frederic Remington with Bill and Has Rasbeck
Great expectations. (Courtesy Remington Art Memorial)

Mrs. Dolph Lynde and Miss Grace Lynde (*with gun*),
Darning Needle Pond

Had not Adirondack Murray called the woods safe and delightful for ladies? (Courtesy
Atwood Manley)

July 10: We got back from the pond about noon. Afternoon we went to chair rock creek fishing. We did not get any.

July 11: Rained by spells this fore noon. Has went with the girls to brandy brook fishing. I went to south creek with Mr Lynd. Caught 2.

July 12: Pleasant and warm. I went with Dolph up the inlet fishing. We caught 2 & came back. Done camp work. Wallace [Guthrie] & Gib went up south creek fishing. They caught about 100 trout.

July 13: Rained a little. About 12 or 1 o clock I took Mr Lynd down the Lake. Grace & John Keeler went with me.

July 14: Pleasant. Mr Keeler, wife, & son, Mrs & Miss Lynde, Has & I went over to Darnkneedle Pond to camp out. I floated Mr Keeler & wife but did not get anything.

July 15: Pleasant but windy. Keeler & party came back. Fred [Remington] came in about 12. Him and Ab [Thompson]. They went off yesterday to Graves Mt & Silver lake [now Lake Marian].

July 16: Pleasant but windy. I stayed about camp all day. Has & Keeler came back from Darnkneedle Pond today. Ab & Fred came back about 12 today.

July 17: I went to Bishops early this morning. The steamer came into our landing after our party and went to the Inlet & Dead Creek, etc. Has, Keeler & wife went to Curtis Pond to stay all night. Mr Remington & wife, Mrs Lynd & daughter went to Bishops to stay all night.

July 18: I went down to Bishops today & back to camp then back to Bishops & stayed home all night. John Keeler came down first trip.

July 19: We broke camp today. Got down about 11.

Telling the writer about that trip, the late Grace P. Lynde said that Remington would float around in Witch Bay with her and Eva Remington perched up toward the prow of the skiff while he sketched or painted with his drawing board resting on the gunwales, and that often he used a big stump out near the point on which to place a small easel. "He'd sit there cross-legged painting, diddling his free foot up and down, up and down, and whistling, whistling, whistling until we all thought we would go mad."

Cranberry was a perfect setting for him to work on the *Hiawatha* order. How much of the lake's wooded shores and scenery he worked into those full-page plates and drawings is anyone's guess, but at least it was there he sketched and painted, diddling his foot and whistling while he worked.

According to the Rasbeck diaries, bear were plentiful during the year 1891. Has and Bill trapped and killed no less than five that year. The other guides at the lake were also successful. The diaries offer a clue to what prompted Remington to make a drawing entitled "A Good Day's Hunting in the Adirondacks," which *Harper's Weekly* used as a middle two-page spread in its January 16, 1892, issue. From old photographs of Has and Bill it is possible to identify them as the two guides seen at the left in this painting, with John Keeler toting a small black bear slung over his shoulders and Remington's uncle Rob Sackrider bringing up the rear as gun-carrier.

The entries in Bill's diary on Remington's 1891 trip to the lake are as follows:

September 24: Mr Sackrider & Fred Remington called for me to go into camp with them at Witch bay. I went to stay till Has came back from Darn Pond. Sam [Bancroft] went after him. Ill stay all night with them. Has went down home to come back in the morning.

September 25: We all went to Darnkneedle Pond to hunt. Has got here to dinner. We got ready & started. Got to Darn camp at 3 or 4. We hunted & killed 3 deer. Fred killed 2 & Mr Sackrider one.

September 26: We skined out our deer & got ready & started for Witch bay camp. Got there about 2 or 3. Got dinner then I got up some wood & came down home. Fred paid me 5 dollars for going with them.

September 27: I went to Sams after my mail & got some bread for Mr Remington & Sackrider then went to Westcott's to grind some coffee then went to camp with the stuff.

September 28: Mr Sackrider & I went to Darnkneedle Pond to hunt. We hunted but did not get anything.

September 29: We all came down to the house & broke camp. Got here at sunset.

September 30: We all stayed near home. Mr Remington & I went to Sams this morning. Afterward Has & Mr Sackrider fished —2.

October 1: We all stayed at the house & shot & had fun. I dug a few potatoes.

Frederic Remington

A Good Day's Hunting in the Adirondacks, by Frederic Remington

Left to right: Has Rasbeck, Bill Rasbeck, John Keeler, and Robert Sackrider. This is from a reproduction which appeared in *Harper's Weekly*, January 16, 1892.

October 2: Now at daylight the party has just gone for Canton. I am packing up to go in camp with the surveyors.

Fred Remington's liking for strong liquor may not be a misleading clue to what constituted fun for that party of four grown men.

The Cranberry outing of 1892 was different. Fred had a big scheme in mind. He dashed off a note to his friend Poultney Bigelow, dated July 26 from New Rochelle, "I am just leaving for a little canoe cruise in the woods for two weeks," and then apparently went directly to the lake after reaching Canton, for Bill Rasbeck entered the following items in his diary:

July 27: I worked for Sam till about 4. Then Fred Remington came in. I stoped to help him.
July 28: I helped Has & Fred off [to the Witch Bay camp].
July 31: Fred & Has came down tonight.
August 1: I went up to bear mt pond to hunt. I got one and got back early.
August 2: I went to bear mt pond agan for beef but did not get any, only got wet. Has & Fred started down the R[iver] this morning.

The last sentence furnishes a preface to what later became a chapter in Remington's first published book, *Pony Tracks* (Harper, 1895), after appearing in *Harper's Monthly* as "Black Water and Shallows." This was his description of the canoe trip he had in mind when writing Bigelow. The cruise itself occupied only four or five days. Remington spent the first of his two weeks on the lake and began the cruise down the Oswegatchie from the dam on August 2. The craft, probably from the shop of his friend J. Henry Rushton, was a sixteen-foot Canadian-style cedar canoe called the *Necoochee*.

People at Cranberry called the scheme impractical. For many miles below the lake the river is shallow and rocky, they pointed out. Even Remington's guide, Has Rasbeck, was among the skeptics, questioning, to begin with, his patron's good sense; and all through the voyage, as they chopped away at obstructing windfalls, smashed against rocks, portaged around long stretches of rapids or waded downstream, slip-

**Frederic Remington
at His Easel**
Buck Island and Bear Mountain
are in the background of this view
from Indian Mountain shore.
(Courtesy Remington Art Memorial)

Cranberry Lake, with Buck Island and Bear Mountain,
by Frederic Remington

This painting, oil on wood, 7″ x 13½″, is of uncertain date (probably in the 1890's). Done on a
shingle and inscribed to one of Remington's friends, it later came into the possession of Irving G.
Vann of Buck Island and is now owned jointly by his descendants. (Courtesy Albert Fowler)

Hung Up, by Frederic Remington   This and the following picture were illustrations for Remington's essay "Black Water and Shallows" in his book *Pony Tracks*.

75

ping and sometimes falling neck deep into holes, Has was "wonderfully cynical at the caprices of the river." A professional guide, he was ready to endure any amount of exertion and fatigue to kill deer or catch trout, but to "go wandering aimlessly down a stream which by general consent was impracticable for boats . . . was a scheme which never quite got straightened out in his mind."

Remington, on the other hand, was in his element. "The river turns, and the ominous growl of the rapids is at hand. . . . No talking now, but with every nerve and muscle tense and your eye on the boil of the water, you rush along. . . . You take it like a hunting-man a six-bar gate. . . . This little episode was successful, but, as you well know, it cannot last. The next rift, and with a bump she is hung upon a sunken rock, and—jump! jump!—we both flounder overboard in any way possible." Knowing that the exertions required in moving down the perverse river his own great bulk, a seventy-pound canoe, provisions for several days, and a cynical guide might not seem like sport to the philosophic mind, Remington takes care to explain the grounds for his "conflagration of ecstasy." The true sportsman can't resist the urge to go "tramping or paddling or riding about over the waste places of the earth, with his dinner in his pocket." He expects "to suffer like an anchorite"; that is part of the program. "He is fighting a game battle with the elements, and they are remorseless." He may break his leg or lose his life in the tip-over, but he is happy—as fit as he will ever be to die.

But love of a fight was only half the explanation of Remington's pleasure in the Oswegatchie trip. There were rewards for the nature lover and the artist too. His eye dilated at "the beautiful quiet of the misty morning on the still water." His nerves tingled at images that rose in the mind's eye as he sat by the campfire at night, images of "birch barks and the red warriors who did the same thing a couple of centuries since." His memory stored up impressions for future drawings and paintings as the forest vistas unrolled:

The long still water is the mental side of canoeing, as the rapid is the life and movement. The dark woods tower on either side, and the clear banks, full to their fat sides, fringed with trailing vines and drooping ferns, have not the impoverished look of civilized rivers. The dark water wells along, and the branches droop to kiss it. In front the gray sky is answered back by the water reflection, and the trees lie out as though hung in the air, forming a gateway, always receding. Here and there an old monarch of the forest has succumbed to the last blow and fallen across the stream. It reaches out ever so far with its giant stems, and the first branch had started sixty feet from the ground. You may have to chop a way through. . . . The original forest tree has a character all its own, and I never see one but I think of the artist who drew second-growth timber and called it "the forest primeval." The quietness of the woods, with all their solemnity, permitting no bright or overdressed plant to obtrude itself, is rudely shocked by the garish painted thing as the yellow polished *Necoochee* glides among them. The water-rat dives with tremendous splash as he sees the big monster glide by his sedge home. The kingfisher springs away from his perch on the dead top with loud chatterings. . . . The crane takes off from his grassy "set back" in a deliberate manner, as though embarking on a tour of Japan, a thing not to be hurriedly done. The mink eyes you from his sunken log, and, grinning in his most savage little manner, leaps away. . . . A stick cracks in the brush, and with all the dash and confidence of a city girl as she steps from her front door, a little spotted fawn walks out on a sedge bank from the alders.

Frederic Remington

The canoeists emerged from the forest and hills into the rural plains. They had dropped eleven hundred feet in fifty-one miles and had run nearly half the course of the Oswegatchie from its outlet at Cranberry to its mouth on the St. Lawrence at Ogdensburg. Above Gouverneur near the hamlet of Emeryville, they were confronted by a river plugged with logs from bank to bank for miles ahead. The spring drive had ended there, and so did Remington's canoe trip. Has still thought the whole thing crazy. But not Remington. The artist's feelings are summed up in the last sentence of his essay: "The zest of the whole thing lies in not knowing the difficulties beforehand, and then, if properly equipped, a man who sits at a desk the year through can find no happier days than he will in his canoe when the still waters run through the dark forests and the rapid boils below."

Black Water, by Frederic Remington

CHAPTER VI

Barney Burns at Brandy Brook

Atwood Manley and Williston Manley

THREE generations of Manleys—Gilbert, his son Williston, and his grandson Atwood—edited the *St. Lawrence Plaindealer* of Canton. Its pages were filled with news and stories of Cranberry Lake for more than fifty years as many of the leading men of Canton went there to hunt and fish. Probably no one has written more extensively on the Cranberry scene than Williston Manley, and it is fortunate that he was reporting for the *Plaindealer* in the great decades around the turn of the century.

In the first section below Atwood Manley gives a brief history of the Barney Burns camp on Brandy Brook, which his father, Williston, and his uncle Mark helped build and where they spent many days fishing. Following this is Atwood Manley's selection (from the *Plaindealer*) of some of his father's best writing on the adventures of those who shared the pleasures of Brandy Brook.

THE BARNEY BURNS CAMP

For a period of seven years, 1894 to 1901, the Barney Burns camp on Brandy Brook was a popular sportsmen's retreat. Fishermen took record trout from the brook, and hunters put out for Bear Mountain Pond directly opposite and some of the best deer hunting on the entire lake.

Like many others from nearby communities, Barney Burns grew up on the fringe of the forest, became a confirmed woodsman, and gravitated to the lake in adult years. By 1887 or earlier Cranberry was the center of his life and remained so till his death in 1901.

"Barney's real interest in Cranberry Lake, at least to begin with and for a good many years," recalled Floyd Rasbeck, "was hounding. Barney dogged deer, hunted them for a living, back in the days when dogging was legal and when the boys at the lake killed for the market. That's what brought him and others to the lake, that and the fishing. Of course in time, and like all the others, he finally turned to guiding. You always found a tub of trout in Barney's spring, and when it came to hounding deer there was none better."

Barney Burns (*right*)

Burns and his party pose at a corner of his lean-to on Brandy Brook. (Courtesy Atwood Manley)

At some time between 1889 and 1893 Barney Burns and the two Manley brothers from Canton, Williston and Mark, became friends. They probably met first at Bishop's, the young men hiring Barney as their guide. Bishop's was the only place on the lake in the eighties where guides were always available, where a feather mattress could be found, and where meals such as the palate seldom savored were served by Auntie B.

In June, 1889, Editor Gilbert Manley stated in the *Plaindealer* that his son Mark had gone to Cranberry for his health and was stopping at Bishop's, that his elder son Williston was also there, and that the fishing was excellent. Williston himself later said that he and Mark became summer regulars at the lake during the early nineties, that Barney Burns was their guide, and that the three of them built the camp on Brandy Brook.

Most woods camps were in those days nothing more than squatters' pre-emption of private or state property. "We didn't have to ask the landlord's permission to select our camp spot," Williston Manley wrote. "The virgin forest was all about. No one asked questions. No one cared. No one thought of titles or deeds." Barney never owned a square inch of the land on which his camp stood, yet he was lord of all he surveyed. From the hour the ice went out in the spring until the lake froze over in late fall, this was his home.

The original camp was a small three-sided structure open on the front to a fireplace. Toward the end of the nineteenth century woodsmen's shelters of this kind, earlier called shanties, became known as open camps or lean-tos. Today, lean-tos built by the State Conservation Department serve campers on the hiking trails and waterways of the Adirondack Forest Preserve. The modern Adirondack lean-to, known throughout the nation and imitated in other park preserves, is an outgrowth of the kind of camp Barney Burns built on Brandy Brook.

The frame of Barney's lean-to was built of logs. Roof and sides were covered with spruce bark. A big log resting on the ground across the front kept the bed of balsam or hemlock

Barney Burns's Camp

. . . after improvements, 1899. (Courtesy Atwood Manley)

Barney's Camp

One of Barney's guests shaves at the washstand, and a corner of the dining room and the hammock may be seen. Courtesy Atwood Manley)

boughs in place and served also as a seat—the deacon seat. The roof had an apron or overhang in front, a feature advanced for the time and now standard.

Barney and the "sports" he guided soon outgrew the original camp. "From a little open camp scarcely large enough for four to lie down in, to something more pretentious . . . an open sleeping shanty, a small cabin, and an open dining room" was Williston Manley's description of the change to larger quarters. The closed cabin had a gabled roof and provided sleeping quarters with bunks. Attached to the rear was a roofed-over, open-sided extension for dining room and kitchen. The uprights, beams, and rafters of this section were unpeeled logs and poles. The whole camp was rustic, down to the homemade tables, bunks, benches, and three-legged camp stools. An added comfort was an old-fashioned rope hammock slung between posts at one end of the dining room. There Barney would lie on an idle afternoon, dangling a leg over the side and reading a year-old issue of *Forest and Stream*.

Oringe Crary of Pierrepont, hunter, self-styled poet and dowser, located the spring at Barney's camp. When told that the camp had no source of drinking water but the brook, Oringe brought his forked divining rod of cherry and with its aid discovered one of the coolest, clearest springs around the lake.

Stories of fabulous catches were still pretty common on Cranberry in the nineties. For example, in 1898, the *Plaindealer* reported that Senator Dolph S. Lynde and John C. Keeler had just returned from a trip to Brandy Brook where Keeler had made one catch of twenty-seven trout which when dressed tipped the scales at thirty-two pounds.

In 1899 Williston Manley made the greatest catch of his life. This came during a trip to Barney's camp that he and his wife Mary made as chaperons to two young unmarried couples. One morning of his stay he decided to take a try at the fishing. He was suffering from a headache and wanted to get off by himself. He tied up to an old knot beside the V Hole

*Barney Burns
at Brandy Brook*

Mary Manley
Mrs. Williston Manley holds her husband's record catch of trout on Barney Burns's dock, 1899. (Courtesy Atwood Manley)

Barney Burns (*at stern*) and Party
A lazy day takes two fishermen among the solitudes. (Courtesy Atwood Manley)

and began trying one fly after another. At the start he had a strike and landed a big one. From then on nothing happened, but he was sure trout were lying in that deep spring hole.

After trying every fly in the book and even the lowly worm, he happened to wash his hands over the side of the boat and notice some tiny punkinseeds swimming about and nibbling at his fingers. He scooped up several, skinned one, and threaded its white-meat body on his hook. Hardly had he tossed the bait overboard when a big trout struck it. Williston never put in such an hour's fishing. When it was over he had seven big speckled beauties on his string. Mary Manley stood on Barney's dock holding that string to be photographed. The smallest of the seven trout dressed weighed two and a half pounds, the largest just under five.

This did not equal in quantity the haul Williston Manley made the first time he tried night fishing on Brandy Brook. That experience and the part his brother Mark played in it became Cranberry Lake history and did much to explain how night fishing on Brandy was discovered. The story was told many years later in one of Williston's "Rounder" columns in the *Plaindealer* in 1923. It is the first of the two following sketches. The second, written in 1899 during Williston Manley's last camping trip on the lake and mailed to his father as easy copy to keep the hook full at the *Plaindealer* office, appeared in the issue of July 26, 1899.

Barney Burns at Brandy Brook

BRANDY BROOK

One summer, my brother got into camp a week before me. One day I received a letter from him. "Come up and I will show you something in the line of fishing that will make your eyes stick out," Mark wrote. The fishing fever was on and I started.

I reached camp late in the afternoon, after a daylight start. We sat around after supper and called the big owls that would respond to our "hoots" and would gradually gather in the tree tops, looking down upon the camp fire. In true woods style, I asked no questions. It got late and finally Barney yawned and rolled into his bunk, but my brother sat on and we chatted. Finally, as I remember it, about eleven o'clock, he got up and stretched himself and looked out at the night. Calm and dark it was, with a liberal sprinkling of stars. "Come on," he said, "and bring your pole." We got into the boat and pulled a few rods above the landing, just up to the Bear Mountain Pond outlet. "Let out your line about the length of your pole," he instructed me. "What will I use for bait?" I asked. "Oh, any old thing, a white miller, or a piece of red rag, anything," he replied; "and then just skitter it along enough to make a little wake," he added.

I skittered it along, or rather, started to skitter it, and something happened out there in the dark that sent a thrill along my backbone down into my toes. It was a regular fellow, the kind they used to lay up against the side of Bishop's old hotel and outline in big black lines for the city sports to look at. I won't go into details regarding the joys of that night. It was one prolonged spasm of bliss. It seemed as though the boat were hovering over a spot where the bottom was lined with big speckled brook trout. Finally, I struck a match and looked down into the bottom of the boat. "This is slaughter. Let's drop back to camp," I offered in an awed tone.

I can tell a fish story with the best of them, but this time I will keep down to the realm of truth. There were probably twenty trout. We did not weigh them, but we were all good judges of trout. I do not believe one of them weighed less than three-quarters of a pound. They scaled up as high as two and a quarter pounds. When I came out of camp that summer, I brought out forty-two trout on ice. One weighed less than a pound. The others ran all the way up to two and a quarter dressed.

We three, Mark, Barney and I, swore ourselves to secrecy. The boats would begin to pull in from the hotel (and there was only one hotel on the lake then, Bishop's) in the morning and the occupants would fish all day, sometimes with good luck and sometimes with poor luck. We three would go out and go through the motions of fishing, but no matter how low our fish tub got, we could replenish it again at night. A good deal depended on the kind of night, but we always caught a few. We figured that they dropped down into the lake, or lower stretches of Brandy Brook, during the day and began to come up to feed about five o'clock, and that only stragglers were caught during the day.

*Barney Burns
at Brandy Brook*

Our bond of secrecy lasted until my brother and I ceased to make our annual trips to Brandy Brook. I suppose Barney had parties in and when the day's fishing was poor, he took them out at night. Anyway, in two or three years, night fishing became popular at Cranberry, and then the supply of trout waned.

Before us stretches Brandy Brook, more of a river than a rivulet, a quiet stream in which the river DeGrasse [Grass] could rest without touching either shore. Just opposite can be seen the outlet to Bear Mountain Pond, the pond itself a short ten-minute paddle from the camp dock. It lies imbedded in Bear Mountain, which rises toward the blue vault above with never a trail to its summit. To the right the brook meanders out of sight amid the dead timber or flow. To the left it reaches out to Cranberry Lake, the "Land of the Loon" and gull, the butt of the winds, the bane of the weary oarsman, and the joy of the timorous deer. Just behind us rise Brandy Brook heights, and beyond them Curtis Mountain, upon the apex of which nestles Curtis Pond, famous for its deer and big trout, which are too sharp to rise to the fly and too dainty to more than nibble at the worm. They are tantalizing but not realizing.

There was a time, and not so long ago, when Cranberry was remote, and wild, and ideal for the man who loves solitude and longs for the forest primeval. Today the shrill toot of four

ATWOOD
MANLEY
AND
WILLISTON
MANLEY

steamers mingles with the cry of the gulls, the creaking of four hotel signs punctuates the droning zephyrs, and of an evening, when silence broods over all, the distant scream of the iron horse mingles with the deep tones of the owl and the weird low call of the loon. Fashion, such as it is, is here, with its shirt waist and pompadour, its outing shirt with boiled collars and cuffs and duck trousers. Money is erecting expensive cottages, bringing in handsome naphtha launches, and making itself generally evident. The days of the open hunting camp on the shores of the lake are waning. The guides cluster more thickly around the hotel veranda to take graceful femininity out for a bluff at fishing, with strict instructions to get it back again out of the wet before the dew may uncrimp its hair. The stump is giving place to the hammock, the hemlock boughs to the hair mattress, combs and brushes are too much in evidence, the good old-fashioned tar dope is succumbing to Lolacapop and similar concoctions, harmless alike to complexion and punkie. And there is a church which the guides have been known to attend.

Cranberry Lake is not a Saratoga. Ten years ago it was a comparative wilderness, with Bishop's old log cabin hotel and a few shanties. Today it is a little village, and in ten years more it promises to rival the Saranacs. Besides Bishop's and Mrs. Bullock's, the past year has seen two new hotels. One lies just across from Bishop's and is run by Dewey and Brooks. The other is at the head of the lake, sheltered behind Buck Island, and its proprietors are Messrs. Nunn and Tucker. It was prophesied when the new hotels went up that they would harm those already established, but such is not the result. More hotels mean more guests, and while Bishop's is still the head-quarters for the large majority, the other hotels are doing a good business. All save the Bullock hostelry have steamers. . . .

The Barney Burns Brandy Brook Camp has become famous to frequenters of the lake. Brandy Brook is the great fishing resort of that region, famous alike for its large number of speckled beauties and . . . for their size. It is the last stream in the world where one would expect to find these delights of the angler. It is sluggish and its waters tepid. Its margins are lined with the unsightly stumps of dead trees standing in many feet of water. . . . But despite dead trees and warm and sluggish waters, Brandy Brook can show more and larger brook trout to the square inch than any other stream in the vicinity. Every year large catches are taken, and every year sees plenty more to take their places. Where they come from, what their number, where they keep themselves, only the tangle of logs can tell. Those captured are the stragglers who wander into these shallower waters for feeding purposes, and the guides will tell you that there are larger fish in the stream than have ever been captured. They are fickle and foxy. On apparently ideal days, and with the right kind of a breeze and with lowering clouds, they may refuse to rise to a fly or touch a worm or bug, a frog or live bait. On other days in some unexpected place the water will begin to boil and great horses will show their glittering sides and fight for a chance to get themselves caught.

Barney Burns at Brandy Brook

It is a skillful angler indeed who can land some of these walloping big beauties. As he makes his glorious, startling plunge for the fly that has not yet touched the water, with perhaps forty or more feet of line between him and the slender tip, it takes a quick, responsive hand and a steady arm to safely hook him. But this is only the commencement. With the five or six-ounce rod bent double; with the silken cord all a-tremor; with that tremor extending along the pole into one's very vitals; with nerve tense, cheeks flushed, and eye aglow; with muscles of the good right arm stiffened yet flexible, alertly following every motion, the battle is on. The line rushes out foot after foot as the splendid fellow makes for some sunken log. Carefully balked, he dashes for liberty up the stream until it seems that line or pole can no longer bear the strain. After what seems ages he is apparently tired out and is carefully led up toward the landing net, only to renew the struggle with refreshed vigor and a fruitless dash beneath the boat. The steady guide holds the boat. If the fisherman is a novice, instructions come from the stern thick and fast; if a veteran, all is silence, the guide preferring to see the fish escape rather than offer advice. At last, the net encloses the speckled sides. He is a beauty and may weigh two, three, four, or even four and a half pounds. It is payment in full for time, hardship, and expense. He may have cost ten dollars per pound. It is cheap. Such is fishing on Brandy Brook.

Barney Burns's camp holds the key to the situation. From it the voice carries to the best fishing grounds. It is miles from the nearest hotel or cottage. Its occupants have their morning's fishing completed before the hotel guests begin to arrive. They do their evening's fishing after they have left.

Nunn's Inn

This photograph was taken at the head of the lake on Indian Mountain shore (about 1900). The Inn was later owned by Indian Mountain Club, and it subsequently became Indian Mountain House. (Courtesy John Aldrich)

Porch of the Cranberry Lake Inn (Bishop's Hotel)
"Fashion, such as it is, is here . . ." (Courtesy John Aldrich)

The editors want to add that the Barney Burns camp was succeeded in 1911 or 1912 by a new camp built by the Indian Mountain Club. This one flourished under its caretaker Jim Cole, who
had lost his right arm just above the elbow, but when the club went
out of business in 1917 it began to decline. Years later a succession
of houseboats were anchored offshore in the flow and served as
floating camps for Brandy Brook fishermen.

CHAPTER VII

The Durston Diary

MARSHALL HOWLETT DURSTON

MARSHALL HOWLETT DURSTON, nephew of Fred Howlett of Tramps Retreat, first visited Cranberry Lake in 1889 as a boy of ten. In 1897, when he was a young man of eighteen, he kept a diary for the period from July 20 to September 1 which he spent at Tramps Retreat. The following excerpts from that diary give a rollicking view of the triangle of camps—Tramps Retreat, Buck Island Camp, Witch Bay Camp—whose residents migrated to Cranberry every summer from Syracuse and Canton, visited back and forth, and fished and hunted together. They included the Howletts and Durstons of Tramps Retreat, the Vanns of Buck Island, and the Keelers and Remingtons of Witch Bay.

This boyhood association with Cranberry was so much a part of Marshall Durston's entire life that when he was in his eighties he recalled its scenes and events as vividly as though he had seen them the day before. In 1960 he elaborated on them in conversations with Albert Fowler, parts of which are set down to supplement the diary.

During the latter part of the nineteenth century there was magic in the name of Howlett at Cranberry Lake. The steamer frequently referred to in the following pages was owned by Bishop and was called the *Howlett*. It did much of its business plying between the hotel and Tramps Retreat and taking Fred Howlett's family and friends on trips and errands around the lake. Both his Durston nephews, Marshall and Dusty, bore the Howlett name. His son, Ames, is often mentioned in the diary.

Tuesday, July 20, 1897: In the A.M. had breakfast with Art at five. Got coffee and lunch at Richland. Met Mr. Vann and Jess at Watertown. Arrived at Benson Mines in a terrible thunder storm. Lady struck next to the hotel. Rode in on stage with Jess and Mr. and Mrs. Remington. Rained a little on way in. Rode up after supper on the steamer. Stopped at Vanns' and the Keelers' cottage. After supper sat around and talked. Uncle Fred was upset about going to N.Y.

Wednesday: In the morning Art Jones and I went up to Toad Pond. Uncle Fred and George went down to Newton Falls. Did not catch anything. Fished for bullheads a little while. Later we went out floating up on the other side of the lake. Did not hear anything. Got in a little after twelve.

Friday: In the P.M. Art and I went up to Olmstead. Left the cottage at two. Got to Olmstead at 4:30. Had a job to find the boat. Went and got wood and supper. Went on the pond at nine. Stayed out until one. Did not hear a deer.

Saturday: In the morning layed in camp in a pouring rain. Peas and tea for breakfast. Left Olmstead at one. Arrived at Toad at three. Fished a little while but did not catch anything. Nelt came up late. Had a game. Reached cottage at five drenched to the spine.

January, 1960: Our trail to Olmstead via Toad started from a point between the Black Duck Hole and the Rasbeck Hole. We kept a boat hidden at Olmstead and had a lean-to there. Uncle Fred used to have George Bancroft or Willard put small bottles of Bass's ale in the roots of trees by the stream on the way to Olmstead so he could refresh himself along the trail on a hot day.

Uncle Fred knew the woods better than the guides. Once he left the Durstons at the Black Duck Hole as they were going up to the lean-to at Olmstead. He told them he wanted to get a deer close to the lake and not have to drag it down from Toad or Olmstead. He said he would be at the big rock at the Olmstead outlet at midnight, not 11:30 or 12:30 but at 12 sharp, and warned them not to point any jacklight at him when he arrived. He was there precisely at midnight and had come all the way after dark and with no trail. He thought nothing of walking from the Black Duck Hole to Nunn's Inn with no trail.

Sunday, July 25, 1897: Had breakfast at eleven. In the P.M. went over to Judge Vann's to see the girls. They all thought I looked like a tramp. Invited to supper but did not stay. Came home and after supper Nelt, Art and I told stories.

Monday: In the morning the crowd came over from the Vanns'. I rowed Fan over to Witch Bay and she paddled to the Vanns'. The crowd played shuffle board before lunch. After dinner we all went in swimming. Afterwards Art and I went to Ash Hill [between Dead Creek Flow and the Inlet]. We did not hear a thing. I fell in four times.

Tuesday: Art and I rowed over to Vann's in the pitch dark. It was very exciting. Quite rough. I had a very nice time indeed with Fan. She and I walked on the piazza.

Saturday: In the P.M. it rained. Art, George, Ames and I played poker in the kitchen. After supper played until eleven. Ames chased Art and I. The hoe handle hit me in the eye. Played with one eye.

Sunday, August 1: Did not get up until late. Elegant day out. After George and Ames went down [to the village] in one boat, Art rowed me down in another. Percy, Art and I walked over to Silver Pond. Percy stole some cookies for Art and I. I rowed Art to Judge Vann's. We all sat around a big bon fire. On the way home I played my instrument and spoiled Vann's and Bess's chance for floating.

Monday: In the morning I went up to the guide's house and studied. Art and Ames went hunting. In the P.M. Art and I went up to Olmstead. When we reached there there were 2 hedgehogs in the camp. We killed both of them. Chopped wood and watched for daylight shot. Got supper and went out on the pond at ten. Floated until 1:30. Did not hear a thing.

Tuesday: Got up at four. Went out and watched but did

not hear anything. Had breakfast at nine. Tried to go to sleep but could not. Left the camp at three very tired indeed. Got down to the cottage at 6:15.

Saturday: In the morning Art and I went across the lake. Art shot a hawk. Uncle Fred cleaned up the cottage. In the afternoon we had a game. I won 85. Later we went over to Keelers'. Art and I raced George and Dusty over. Uncle Fred sent George after some remedies for Mr. Remington. After supper sang songs and sent up a balloon. On the way home sent up Roman candles.

January, 1960: Frederic Remington stayed at the Witch Bay Camp in a one-story house with just a door and two windows. It had a fine view from a knoll seventy-five or one hundred yards down the shore from Merrill's [now Cole's] Point toward Deremo's. I stayed there one night, and the place was overrun by mice. Remington used to throw his whiskey bottles back of the camp, but not far enough that they could not be seen. [The Witch Bay Camp, unlike the large, two-story structures at Tramps Retreat and Buck Island, consisted of two log lean-tos built on opposite sides of a huge rock as well as the small one-story cottage and an occasional tent.] One time he came over to Tramps Retreat and found the liquor which had been hidden against his arrival. He also found some Roman candles and chased Mrs. Remington about the place, setting off fireworks close behind her. He was a big man, broad shouldered, with thick muscular thighs. He played on the Yale football thirteen before the eleven came in. His typical day at the lake was to get up about 1 P.M., have three drinks, lunch, a couple of cigars, start painting about 3 P.M., and work till midnight. Then he would get thoroughly liquored up. He drank himself to death before he was much more than forty [Remington's death at forty-eight is usually attributed to complications resulting from a ruptured appendix].

Uncle Fred, like Remington, hastened death by drink and

high living. He should have been trained as a doctor as he wanted to be, but his father tried to make a first-class banker of him. He got into several businesses that lost him money.

Sunday, August 8: After breakfast Art, Dusty and I picked berries. At noon the Keelers and the Vanns came over here to dinner. After dinner we sat around. Later the steamer came up and brought me a letter. The crowd from Keelers' stayed to supper. After supper we sang songs and set off fire-works.

The Durston Diary

Witch Bay Camp, about 1897

Has and Bill Rasbeck and Mrs. John Keeler are seated at the table; Mr. Keeler and his three sons are in the center foreground; the women at the right and left are unidentified. Frederic Remington shared this camp with the Keelers and the Lyndes and enjoyed the marvelous view across the lake to East Mountain. (Courtesy Mrs. Benjamin Keeler)

Tramps Retreat

Built in 1886 by A. A. Howlett and A. H. Hiscock, the camp housed three generations of Howletts. The son, Fred Howlett, was the one best known to Cranberry Lake. After the grandson Ames tried in vain to cure his tuberculosis by living there all year round, the camp was sold to the Moore family in 1916. This view, taken in the late 1930's, shows one of the daughters, Edith Moore Ellison, on the porch steps. The camp was destroyed by lightning and fire in April, 1957. (Photo by Walter Ellison)

Mr. Remington was feeling happy when he left here. We found a mouse nest in the box of fireworks. We had at dinner: Mr. and Mrs. and Dillaye Vann, Mr. and Mrs. Boldin, Mr. and Mrs. Keeler and Remington, Mr. Will Twitchel and Charlotte Wilkinson and Sutton.

Wednesday: In the morning got up at eight and had Percy hear my Latin. After breakfast we had a game. I won a little. Art and I sailed down to Lone Pine. In the P.M. went down to Bullocks and Rasbecks. In the evening Percy walked down with me to church, but we were late. Later we went down to Bullocks' to a dance, and stayed until 12.

January, 1960: One afternoon I started about 3:30 to row down to Bishop's for supper, but when I got there I was told it was too late for supper and that I could get all I wanted to eat at MacAleese's at the Windfall. So I went over and found a square dance in progress with people coming from as far as Benson Mines. Ab Thompson in a Prince Albert coat was playing the violin, and Mac was strumming the banjo. I danced till midnight, when there was lemonade and beans. Then danced till six-thirty, when I started back to the lake on a buckboard. The king bolt broke on the shaft, and we had to walk. I arrived at Tramps Retreat at 11:30 A.M. and slept around the clock.

The Durston Diary

Saturday: Father Clune and Uncle Fred left at 6:30 for Bishop's. Art, Ames and I went in swimming but the steamer came. Made dinner out of breakfast. After dinner Uncle Fred came up on the scow of bricks. We all unloaded the bricks. Afterwards I went up to the guide's house and studied. Dusty went up to Ash Hill and shot a doe. Will Peck rode up on the steamer. We had a game. Uncle Fred came and played for 14 and won 146. I lost 55.

Sunday, August 15: In the morning Uncle Fred shot off his blame cannon at six. Dusty and George went up to Ash Hill and got his deer. Art and I rowed Uncle Fred and Ames over to Judge Vann's. We had a chewing match [argument] on the way. After dinner we all went in swimming. Dusty and Will Peck dove from the rock. Afterwards we went over and made our dinner call at the Keelers'. Dusty, Ames, Art and Uncle Fred had a water fight in the boat. This day has not seemed much like Sunday.

Monday: In the morning we went over to Bear Mountain, Buck and Joe Indian Island on a hand drive. Art and I had to row Ames, Dusty, and Uncle Fred all the morning in a hard wind. I got all twisted around on Joe Injun. Mr. Keeler, Judge Vann, Dillaye and Will Peck were here to dinner and stayed until about five. In the evening Nelt and Mr. Burden came in from hunting and stayed all night. We had a great game of poker until one o'clock. I won 47. Held 4 8's against Dusty's king.

Wednesday: In the morning studied up by the wood pile. The Captain brought up Deacon White and M. Lowry. Ames, Art and I ran the steamer and got a great necker [tongue-lashing] from Uncle Fred.

Thursday: Ames and Art went to the lick about five. I got up at 7:30 and prepared the breakfast. The steamer came up before breakfast with the Misses Page, Dr. and Mrs. Sears and Uncle Fred. They brought up a dozen chickens.

The Vann Camp on Buck Island, about 1917

Built in 1895, this spacious camp was the summer home of Judge and Mrs. Irving G. Vann for many years, and has been occupied by six generations of the family. This view was taken around 1917. (Photo by Fay Welch)

January, 1960: We had a raised platform above the deer lick back of Tramps Retreat. We used to go up to the lick (there was no trail of course) and, after looking out to see that Rip Leonard, the game warden, was not around, wait on the platform in the dark for deer, then open the jack to light up the animal for a shot.

Uncle Fred helped put an end to using hounds for deer by persuading the guides they were scaring away the game.

In 1895 a forest fire burned from Benson Mines to within four miles of Tramps Retreat. We had to keep wet blankets on the roof against the hot embers falling all around us.

Saturday: Dr. and Mrs. Sears, the Misses Page, Peck, Mr. Sax and I went up to Brandy Brook on a picnic. After dinner I took Miss Page out rowing up to the head of the brook. Went back to the camp and stayed a while. Steamer took me over to the mouth of the Inlet. Got supper for Dusty and Ames. After supper Uncle Fred and George came with my tobacco. He tried to jump on me about staying down to the hotel. Had a small game in the evening.

Sunday, August 22: In the morning I dressed up in several different costumes and Uncle Fred pushed me off the dock. Afterwards he, Dusty and I went in swimming. Dusty dove for my cuff and got it. We went over and said good-bye to the Vanns. After supper we built a fire and set off fire-works. Uncle Fred jollied Miss Page. Made lots of noise on way up from hotel on the steamer and Uncle Fred tried to give us a necker.

Monday: In the morning helped Captain load up steamer. In the evening rode Captain's wheel down after the mail. Built another fire and popped corn. Filled Miss Page's bed with corn and chewed Sax's clothes.

Wednesday: Lady of the Lake took us up to the cottage with Mrs. Lyons on board. Percy and I went down to the hotel and so did Dusty and George. I took Dodie out rowing up the lake and floated back. Had a very large time.

The *Howlett*

Named for Fred Howlett, the boat was a wood-burning steamer owned by Riley Bishop. It did much of its business plying between Bishop's Hotel and Tramps Retreat and transporting Fred Howlett and his family and guests around the lake. (Photo by Ivan Bancroft)

January, 1960: Over the bar in the log cabin of Bishop's Hotel Frederick Remington painted a picture of a five-pound trout. In the trout's open mouth he drew a jigger glass and marked it BAIT.

The original door at Tramps Retreat was in one piece and was paneled inside with two vertical panels. One contained the menu of the first meal served at Tramps Retreat, replete with imported wines. Inscribed on the other were the signatures of famous guests—Frederic Remington, Irving Bacheller [author of *Eben Holden* and other fiction, who grew up on a farm near Canton and frequently vacationed on or near

Cranberry Lake in adult life], Chester S. Lord [managing editor, New York *Sun*], etc. Between the two panels was written the story of the panther Uncle Fred saw at Toad Pond and couldn't shoot because George Bancroft had his gun.

This one-piece door was later replaced by a Dutch door which made the living room much lighter. The Durston family took the original door down to Syracuse and stored it in their stable for years. It was finally stolen.

Sunday, August 29: Got up early and started the fire. After breakfast Sport, Peck and I went down to Dewey's and Bishop's. I rowed down. Took dinner at Sam's. Dodie came over for a little while in the morning. She was icy while Peck and I were at Dewey's. Mary gave me some milk and cookies which I ate down cellar. After supper I went over to see Dodie and had a very nice time. Very rough coming back.

Monday: In the morning Percy and I rode up on the steamer with the Stewarts and Mr. Cole. We went over to Brandy Brook, Judge Vann's, and up to the cottage. Dodie and I sat on the back and sang songs. Said good-bye to Dodie and the rest. After dinner studied. The steamer came up with a load of brick. In the evening Peck and I dressed up and went down to Bishop's. Floated down by Green Bay. Percy and Ames went up the lake for deer. George went up to the lick.

Tuesday: In the morning Peck and I went in to the breakfast table with our crazy suits on. I thought the people would die laughing at us. Went up to George's and down to Sam's. Rode up on the steamer with the Morgans and Gubers. Stopped and went through the Boyd cottage. Took our farewell swim which was very cold. Mr. Knox of Hermon was here to dinner. In the P.M. packed my clothes and shaved. Rode down on the steamer with the Boyds. Ames had powder blow up in his face. Uncle Fred came. Had a chewing match with him on the steamer on the way down to the Dam. Told Willard and Charlie. Swiped some jam and apples.

MARSHALL
HOWLETT
DURSTON

Wednesday, September 1: Got up at 6:30. Had breakfast at Bishop's. Said good-bye to all at dear old Cranberry. Rode out with Fraser and White from Buffalo and Chicago. Arrived at Newton Falls at 11. Played piano and sang before and after dinner. Left Falls at 1:45. Had a pleasant trip. Left Fraser and White at Carthage. Arrived at Watertown at 5:30. Walked up the street and met Irene. Flirted with the Miller girls. Left Watertown six-thirty. Arrived home in Syracuse at 9:45 with Chan Day and Bill Nye. Marcia, Aunt Belle, Lizzie, May and Will Peck were here.

CHAPTER VIII

The Hardwood Mill

CYRIL BACKUS CLARK

CYRIL BACKUS CLARK, a retired vice-president of the American Cyanamid Company, lived in Canton as a boy when his father formed the firm of Clark and Squires to lumber in the Cranberry Lake area, first on the Grass River and then on the Oswegatchie River, where the Hardwood Mill was located a few miles below the lake. Most of his information centers around the year 1904, when he worked at the mill with his cousin Roscoe Backus and kept a diary of his activities. He also draws on an account of these early days that he wrote during the 1940's for his children and grandchildren. He called on his cousin to help fill out some of the gaps when he gathered the scattered material together for this chapter, and it is to their careful and combined efforts that we owe the finished article.

Two rivers, the Oswegatchie and the South Branch of the Grass, supplied the main channels for lumbering in the early days in the Cranberry Lake area, and the firm of Clark and Squires used both of them in its operations. On the Grass River it floated pulp to the paper mill at Pyrites and softwood lumber logs to the Canton Lumber Company mill at Canton. It pulled hardwood by horse to its own mill on the Oswegatchie at the foot of Buck Mountain, four and a half miles below the dam at Cranberry Lake.

It is interesting to trace the gradual climb of lumber mills up these two rivers from the St. Lawrence, beginning with the first mill erected in St. Lawrence County at the mouth of the Oswegatchie in 1751 by Father Picquet. The French called the stream *Rivière de la Présentation,* while the Indians called it *Soegatzy.* My father's story was that in the early days an old Indian was crossing the river when his horse got away from him. After a hard struggle he caught the animal again and exclaimed, "Horse we got ye," and thus christened the river. Picquet's sawmill was small and was operated by water power furnished by a dam. It supplied lumber for building in the immediate neighborhood. This type of mill was later common to most towns in the county.

Settlement along the two rivers can be traced by the dates when sawmills were first put up. On the Oswegatchie the course is about like this: Ogdensburg, 1751; Heuvelton, 1807; Gouverneur, 1809; Fullerville, 1813; Edwards, 1818; Fine, 1834; and the village of Oswegatchie, shortly after 1889 when the railroad reached there. On the Grass River there was a sawmill at Massena in 1792, at Madrid in 1802, Russell in 1806, Clifton (Clarksboro) in 1866, and Newbridge in 1909. Around 1904 there was a steam mill at the foot of Cranberry Lake, and the only other one in the area was the Hardwood Mill on the Oswegatchie.

By this time the Canton Lumber Company had a substantial frame building on the Grass River at the Windfall. This was designated on the old maps as the Canton Lumber Company Farm. (It was later owned and operated by Bill Mac-Aleese.) Logs cut in the summer were put on skids, drawn to skidways on the river in winter, and floated down to the mills during high water as soon as the ice went out in the spring. These logs were mostly pine, spruce, and balsam.

As the Oswegatchie flows out of Cranberry Lake, its direction is west, but after a little more than a mile it curves around and goes north till it nears   k's. Then it turns west again to skirt the north side of Buck   ntain, and after another mile and a half reaches the Hardw   Mill. It continues on west of the mill to the outlet of Tooley   d and then swings south along the west side of Buck Mountain to the drowned lands produced by the dam erected at Newton Falls by the Newton

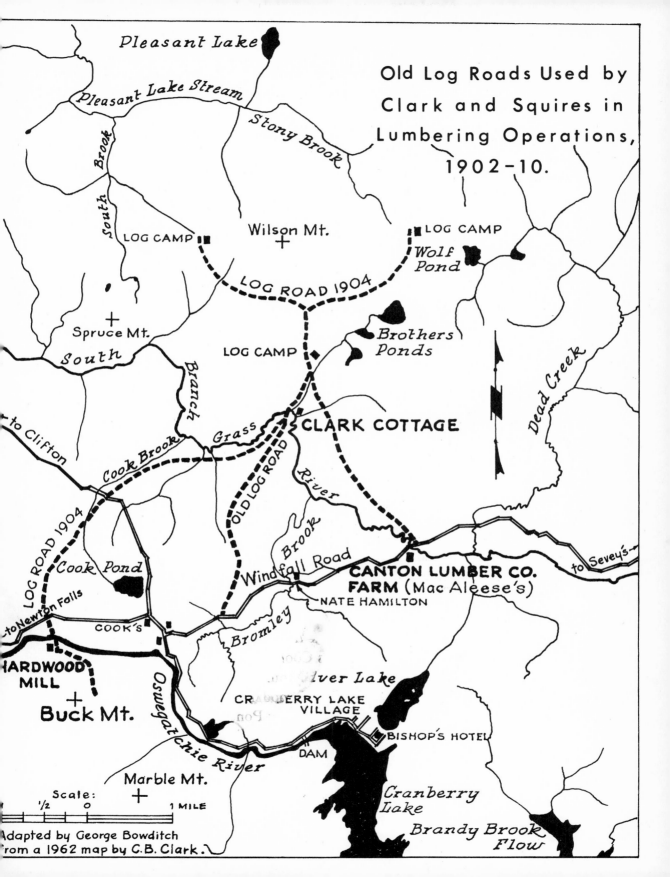

Old Log Roads Used by
Clark and Squires in
Lumbering Operations,
1902-10.

Pleasant Lake

Pleasant Lake Stream

Stony Brook

South Brook

Wilson Mt.

LOG CAMP

LOG CAMP

Wolf Pond

LOG ROAD 1904

Spruce Mt.

South

Branch

LOG CAMP

Brothers Ponds

Dead Creek

Grass

CLARK COTTAGE

Cook Brook

OLD LOG ROAD

River

to Clifton

LOG ROAD 1904

Cook Pond

Brook

Windfall Road

CANTON LUMBER CO.
FARM (MacAleese's)

to Sevey's

to Newton Falls

COOK'S

Bromley

NATE HAMILTON

HARDWOOD
MILL

Buck Mt.

Oswegatchie River

Silver Lake

CRANBERRY LAKE
VILLAGE

BISHOP'S HOTEL

DAM

Marble Mt.

Scale:

½   0   1 MILE

Cranberry
Lake

Brandy Brook
Flow

Adapted by George Bowditch
from a 1962 map by C.B. Clark.

CYRIL
BACKUS
CLARK

Falls Paper Company in the 1890's. From the dam at Cranberry Lake to the dam at Newton Falls the river drops only fifty feet in nine miles. I have rowed a boat from the Falls to the Hardwood Mill.

The dam and the paper mill at Newton Falls were built in 1894 under the direction of James Outterson for James L. Newton, who owned a tract of about fifteen thousand acres of neighboring forest land. Up to that time there was no settlement of any kind in the area, and the waterfall was seldom visited except by hunters. Work was rushed on an extension of the railroad from Benson Mines five miles away because the machinery for making paper could not be brought in over the

Cranberry Lake Village, about 1910
The Catholic church and the village schoolhouse are prominent in the picture. (Courtesy John Aldrich)

rough lumber roads. The Newton Falls Paper Company was organized the same year, 1894. The control of its properties subsequently passed into the hands of International Paper Company and later of McGraw-Hill, Inc., and Chilton Company, joint owners today. It is now the Newton Falls Paper Mill, Inc.

My father, Cyrus F. Clark, had many dealings with the Newton Falls Paper Company when he was operating the Hardwood Mill, and I drew a lot of our lumber from the mill to the railroad at Newton Falls, where it was shipped to market. In my diary for 1904 there is this entry for July 5: "Edson Clark and I came up on the train to Newton Falls. Got to mill and went to loading lumber. Took care of our horses and got through at nine." The entry for July 6 reads: "Got up at five, fed our horses, and then ate breakfast. Made one trip all right to the Falls and then one in the afternoon. Got back home and got work done by 9 P.M." It was five miles from the mill to the railroad at Newton Falls, and we were supposed to make two trips a day.

My entry for July 7 records one of the hazards of the road. "In the afternoon Ed came up and rode with me and his horses tipped his load over." Another difficulty shows up July 8. "We make one trip. I am sick and unable to go in the afternoon. I sleep and rest. It was on account of the heat." On July 9 we made two trips against odds: "Mosquitoes and Punkies are thick as the devil." But Sunday brought its rewards on July 10. "We got up about eight. We go to Cranberry Lake. Stay until about 3 P.M. We have sundies and one bottle of birch beer. We get home, after eating ice cream and candy, about five."

July 12 brought on something of a crisis. "I start to make my trip and get about one half of a mile when one of my old horses played out and I unhitched her and started to come back to the Mill, when she dropped dead." In my income account I find I made two trips a day for four days and received $1.50 a day and board. The day my horse died I got nothing except my board. Uncle Juddy Backus, the superintendent of the mill, used to wake us up around four o'clock by yelling, "Come on, get out of there. You'll get bedsores." From this I figure the work day was from 4 A.M. to 9 P.M., or seventeen hours.

On a little knoll overlooking the Oswegatchie just below the dam and bridge by the mill, Dad had built a very comfortable log cottage for his family and friends. It had a large front porch where you could sit and enjoy the view if you did not mind the smudge necessary to drive away the mosquitoes, punkies, and black flies. This was headquarters for either Clark or Squires or both when they were at the mill.

The mill was a couple of hundred feet up the river, and beyond it, a little back from the river, was the log stable for the horses. Tracks for the sawed lumber trucks led off to the south and were lost among great piles of lumber. Solid woods were all around us. It was about half a mile out to the Newton Falls–Windfall–Cranberry Lake road. The only house toward Newton Falls was a hunting camp owned by a man named Balderson on the outlet to Tooley Pond. Nearby my uncle Silas Clark built a camp on the Oswegatchie which he used for several years. Toward Cranberry Lake about a mile and a half there were two hotels and one house. Cook's Hotel stood near Cook Pond where the Newton Falls road joined the road from Clifton, and a little farther on was the Thomas House where the old Windfall road turned off to the left and wound across the Windfall to Sevey's. Jack Thomas had a house between the two hotels, and Silas Cook lived in his hotel. They made most of their money from their bars, and most of the pay earned by the lumbermen found its way into these two saloons. Clifton was twelve miles to the north through the woods, and Cranberry Lake three miles to the southeast. East on the Windfall road, three miles from Cook's, was Nate Hamilton's old log cabin, and a little farther on near the Grass River was MacAleese's.

We had a lot of company at the mill and a good deal of fun. One day a bunch of us went up to Cranberry Lake, took the steamer *Wanakena* to Nunn's for dinner, and then went

The *Wanakena*

Owned by the Rich Lumber Company, the vessel stands at the dock at Nunn's Inn. (Courtesy John Aldrich)

on to Wanakena. We visited back and forth with Uncle Silas at his camp, going by the road or by boat on the river. My diary for July 23, a Saturday, shows that Uncle Frank, Dad, and I played pedro most of the day. Sunday morning we hitched up the horses and drove to Cranberry to church, and in the afternoon we had a songfest and Dad told deer stories. On Monday I was put on the job of "tailing" the mill—taking care of the slabs and boards as they came from the saw. This must have done me up, for I laid off the rest of the week. July 27 saw four of us going raspberrying and getting sixteen quarts. When we got home I made ice cream. A few days later we

CYRIL
BACKUS
CLARK

went blueberrying on the Windfall and got two bushels. I picked eighteen quarts. The next week I worked every day but one, and in a single day of tailing the mill I handled twenty-seven thousand feet of lumber, about fifty tons. I was tired at the end of that day.

Driving logs was the most interesting thing I did at the mill. I did this several summers and got so I could break jams and ride logs pretty well. We used calked boots and pikepoles some fifteen feet long. During the summer of 1905 my cousin Roscoe Backus and I were given the job of bringing down the logs which had been hung up along the shore, caught on branches or rocks or run aground in the three miles of river above the mill. The first thing we did was to fill the thick soles of our heavy shoes with half-inch calks. Armed with pikepoles, we set out to drive logs. We carried our lunch, including a maple syrup can full of tea made by the camp cook that was strong enough to float an egg. We walked up to Cook's and up the Cranberry Lake road to an old dam where the logs had been rolled in off a skidway. There we were joined by a Windfall character usually found hanging around Cook's bar. I never knew his name, but we called him Swamp Ox. In the rapids below the old dam was a large pile of logs hung up by rocks in the center of the river and backing up the water for some distance. Our first job was to break this jam.

In a regular spring drive in rough water the river drivers used dynamite to blow out the key log if they were not able to break the jam with peaveys, pikes, and axes. We did it with pikes and peaveys. The trick was to get to shore quickly after the jam started to move, or you might have to ride it down to still water. There was considerable risk of a quick end if you fell into the churning water full of speeding logs. Our drive was child's play compared to the big ones on the Grass River, but it was interesting and exciting to two young boys.

Swamp Ox amused us by loosening a log in the rapids and sitting astride it with his legs locked underneath and floating down the rapids with the log cross-stream. He was smoking his old clay pipe all the while. He would have reached still water safely if the log had not hit a submerged stone which gave it a roll and alternately put him under and out and under again till he was nearly drowned. We were a week or two getting all the stray logs down to the sorting gap by the mill.

Some days the going was easy and lots of fun. In the still water we floated along on a raft made by nailing or tying two logs together. All we had to do when tailing the drive was to loosen and start on their way the logs caught on the banks or hung up on rocks. Where the current was slow, life was leisurely, and we told stories and sang songs. One of the songs still stays with me. I probably learned it from Swamp Ox. It had many verses, most of them unprintable, and started out like this:

> I am a cow puncher;
> I am going to quit.
> I hain't got a dollar,
> And I don't care a bit.
>
> (*Chorus*)
> And it's whoop de hoop
> De oodle doodle do.
> And it's whoop de hoop
> De oodle doodle do.
>
> Here's little Sally Walker;
> She's a fine little squaw.
> She lives on the bank of
> The big Wabash-a-ta.

The next fifteen or twenty verses recite the adventures of the cowboy and little Sally Walker in language customary to Cook's bar on a Saturday night after payday.

The sorting gap was about half a mile above the mill. In the middle of the river was a string of booms held together at the ends by chains and held to the middle of the river by log piers made like corncribs and filled with stone. At the sorting gap logs belonging to different companies were held back of the booms to be sorted out and either sent downstream to the mill at Newton Falls or put in the Hardwood Mill pool.

CYRIL
BACKUS
CLARK

Cutting logs was usually done by contract. After the contractor or jobber had cut and skidded his logs, they were scaled to determine how many board feet they contained. The scaling was done mostly by Uncle Juddy Backus. It consisted of measuring the diameter and length of the log and then consulting statistical tables which gave the board feet of sawed lumber. At the same time the logs were marked for identification with a tool called a marker, which looked like a sledge hammer but which had in its head a distinguishing design raised in relief, so that a blow on the end of a log would leave an imprint in the wood. Two or three marks were usually made near the outer edge of the log so they could be seen as the log floated in the water.

One summer my cousin and I sorted logs. The logical method was to walk up the old log road to the sorting gap, but this was too tame for us and we took the more exciting and wetter route of walking the booms from the mill to the gap. The booms were full-length trees, big at the butt and dwindling down to almost nothing at the top, and frequently the small end was under water or would go under water as we ran over it. All the pulpwood was floated down the river to Newton Falls, and all the hardwood was hauled direct to our mill, but the softwood lumber logs had to be carefully scaled, marked, and separated. Some were sent down to the Falls and some kept for the Hardwood Mill.

Below the mill was a dam made of logs with plank facings on the upstream side. In the middle was a sluiceway through which most of the water flowed and the logs were sluiced down river. The drop through the dam was some six or seven feet, with a further drop of a foot or two through the rapids just below the dam. This dam backed up the water for quite a distance, and it was still water for a mile and a half upstream nearly to Thomas's on the Windfall.

One of the jobbers for Clark and Squires was Warren Guinup. He had a lumber camp at the east slope of Buck Mountain near the Old Forge Dam. My cousin Roscoe Backus remembers Warren Guinup as a dapper young man, always neat and well dressed. A jobber hired his own men and built his own camps on the small tract assigned to him for the work of cutting logs and piling them on skidways. He got his camp supplies on credit from the store at the Hardwood Mill. Manager Backus assigned the sections to be cut, furnished the supplies from the store, supervised and measured the logs cut and the hemlock bark peeled, and gave the proper credits to the jobber.

At the Old Forge Dam half a mile above Cook's Hotel on the Oswegatchie, in swift water, one of our logs drove one end under the crossbeam in the dam, and the other end stuck up above water upstream. Other logs piled up and the log drive came to a stop. A man was sent to the mill for sticks of dynamite, caps, and fuses. Some twenty sticks of dynamite were tied on the end of a ten-foot pole. The fuse was lighted and the pole was jammed down under the big log. Some of the logs went up in the air as high as the tops of the trees, and so did the crossbeam of the dam. The jam moved along down river, but the dam was cleaned out down to the river bed and was never rebuilt. It had been a floodwater dam over the run of rapids.

My father was a businessman and had operated a country store at North Russell and a group of seven butter and cheese factories in Russell before he moved to Canton. When he came to Canton he became manager and director of the Canton Cooperative Insurance Company. All these activities were carried on together with his lumbering. But he never seemed to let his business interfere with his pleasure. Perhaps his desire to make money in the lumber business was secondary to his love of being in the woods and hunting and fishing. His father, as a buyer of furs, traveled all through the foothills of the Adirondacks and hunted and fished in this area.

Father had had considerable experience in lumbering in

The Hardwood Mill

Russell and Clare before he moved to Canton in 1889 and joined his cousin to form the firm of Clark and Squires. Almeron Z. Squires, the elder of the two, was educated at St. Lawrence University. He studied law, was admitted to the bar in 1869, and, after eight years as professor of mathematics at his alma mater, practiced law in Canton. He served as special surrogate for ten years.

Most of the lumbering carried on from the Hardwood Mill was on or around Buck Mountain. I remember working with an old Frenchman cutting and skidding logs between the mill and Balderson's on the north side of the road. We had a horse for drawing the logs to the skidways. While I was trimming up a big spruce tree we had felled, my double-bitted ax glanced off and went into the top of my foot. The old Frenchman got my shoe off, put me on the horse, took a cud of tobacco out of his mouth and slapped it into the cut, put a piece of my sock around it, and led me back to the mill. I still have the scar from that mishap.

The river was full of pulpwood and softwood logs above the dam. As boys, we enjoyed running across the logs in the mill pond. We tried to run across the pulpwood, but it was too small to hold us up and we fell in the water. When I was first at the mill in 1904, there were big piles of hardwood logs on the bank upstream from the mill. These had been cut on Buck Mountain and drawn down during the winter. When they were rolled into the water, it was very difficult to get them over to the dragline to pull them up into the mill. Many would sink, and it was necessary to spear them with pikepoles and drag them along to the point where they would be caught by the lugs on the chain hoist.

One of the mill buildings that was of particular interest to me as a boy was the storehouse. It was really a small country store, containing a variety of hearty foods such as pork and beans, potatoes, flour, and all kinds of canned goods. It had to carry quite extensive supplies for the lumbering needs of twenty-odd men at the mill and the various contractors on the

Grass and Oswegatchie. I remember that one year there was a lot of succotash left over, and we had it at home in Canton so long that I have never liked the stuff since. The store stocked lard, salt pork, bacon, maple syrup, the makings for pancakes, axes, saws, log chains, pikepoles and peaveys, feed for a dozen horses, harness parts, axle grease, parts for the mill, lubricating oil, and miscellaneous tools.

The entire clearing for the mill buildings was about four acres. Much of it was used for storing the lumber, which was run out on small cars pushed by hand along wooden tracks. The lumber was carefully stacked in piles ten or twelve feet high, each layer separated from the one below by crosspieces, with a gentle slope to help the rain run off. The lumber was left to dry out and season before we drew it by horse and wagon to Newton Falls to be shipped to market by train.

The mill itself was a large steam affair with power furnished by two boilers fired with sawdust and waste slabwood. It was two stories high and about sixty feet long and thirty feet wide. It had the usual barn-shaped roof and was covered with tar paper. An extension to the east housed the two boilers, each with a high steel stack sticking up through the roof. There was a steam whistle above this roof to call the men to work. The capacity of the mill was twenty-five to thirty thousand board feet a day. Clark and Squires bought the mill as a going concern. It was formerly known as the Pearly Waite Mill, probably the first commercial hardwood mill in the area.

I liked to watch the sawyer at work. He was the most important man at the mill. In 1904 Andrew Negus was the sawyer. He was an old and experienced hand who knew how to get the best out of crooked logs, knotty logs, and logs with various defects. By the way he placed the log on the carriage and the way the cuts were made, he determined the quantity and character of the lumber produced by the big circular saw and the amount of waste discarded as slabwood. It was fascinating to me to watch the log run up to the big saw, the cutting of a perfect plank, the quick return of the carriage, the quick

The Hardwood Mill, 1910

Roscoe J. Backus stands beside a carriage at the Mill. (Photo by Cyril B. Clark)

forcing forward of the log for the next cut by the carriage man, and the almost instantaneous return of the log to the saw. Andrew Negus had three men to keep his sawing operations in full swing: one who got the logs from the pond and helped load them on the carriage; one who rode the carriage, anchored the log on the carriage, and moved it forward with levers; and one who tailed the saw, as I did on occasion. Additional hands on the edge trimmers and other jobs brought the total at the mill to about twenty men.

My grandfather Cornelius Backus, of Russell, used to tell me bear stories. The Backus family came to St. Lawrence County from Royalton, Vermont, in 1819. Grandpa Backus was built like Santa Claus or Grover Cleveland, whom he much admired. His short legs and big stomach made sitting on his lap a rather precarious experience, but I sat there listening to his bear stories and smelling the odor of homemade tallow candles. The story I remember best is about Willard Howland, an old Cranberry Lake guide and hunter whose house two miles south of Russell on the Degrasse-Russell road was often pointed out to me.

One day when Willard was out hunting, he came into a clearing. He leaned his gun up against a big pine stump and sat down to rest. As he sat there, he heard something inside the stump. So he climbed up the stump and looked down in. There were two little black bear cubs. He jumped down into the stub and sat there playing with the cubs. After a while he decided to get out, but there was nothing to hang onto. It looked as if he would have to stay there till someone found him. While he was pondering his fix, he heard a scratching and growling and, looking up, saw the old mother bear glaring down at him. Well, as Willard said later, he thought he was a goner. Still growling, the old bear turned around and started backing down into the stub, getting nearer and nearer to Willard. When the bear was almost at the bottom, Willard got out his knife, grabbed the bear by the tail, jabbed the bear with the blade, and, would you believe it, that old bear pulled Willard right out of the stump.

Around 1900 there were still many stages operating in St. Lawrence County. These were generally double buggies with a team of horses, and they usually carried passengers, freight, and mail to the hinterland from points along the railroads. One of them ran from Newton Falls to Cranberry Lake when we were at the Hardwood Mill. One day I got a letter from my mother delivered to me at the mill by the stage. It asked: "Are the Indians cross when they are drunk? I believe I should be afraid of them." A lot of Indians worked in the area during the lumbering season. I learned to count in what was supposed to be good Indian. Up to fifteen it went like this: *een, teen, tither, fether, fix, satha, latha, cora, dora, dix, eeenabob, teenabob, titherbob, fetherbob, jigger.*

We had two types of horses in the woods, small light ones for driving and big Western ones for lumbering and hauling. It was a small light horse hitched to a single buggy that Roscoe drove the forty miles from the Hardwood Mill to Canton in eight hours with me on the seat beside him after I had cut my foot. One day when I was sixteen I walked that forty miles from Canton to the mill, the last twelve miles through the solid woods and after dark. I was so scared of bears and panthers that I ran most of the way. The next day the calves of my legs were so sore that I could hardly walk.

Weekends the men from the mill always went up to Cook's and got drunk. The result was that we were short a few men on Monday mornings. One Saturday night around ten o'clock just as Roscoe and I were ready to turn in, some of the men came back a little the worse for Cook's liquor and said that Joe was out at the main road in the ditch and couldn't walk in. Roscoe and I got a wheelbarrow and started out to the road to bring him in. We found him in the ditch all right, dead to the world. We hoisted him into the wheelbarrow, and with much wheezing and puffing interspersed with snores from Joe, we wheeled him back to camp and deposited him in the bunkhouse.

A fellow by the name of Sandy Avery worked in the mill. He seemed to be a gentleman, never drank, wore a big watch and chain, and always had money in his pocket. Between Thomas's Saloon and Cook's Hotel on the Windfall there was a depression and a culvert. One night as Uncle Juddy was driving over this culvert in pitch blackness, he heard someone say, "Shut up, damn you." There were often fights and drunks in that section, and he paid little attention to what he heard. Next day Sandy was found dead, and his watch and money were gone. That was all. No action was taken. That was the way of the woods at the time.

Before they bought the Hardwood Mill, Clark and Squires had started lumbering operations on an eight-thousand-acre tract on the Grass River and hired Uncle Juddy to manage the operations there. He went down to the Indian reservation at Hogansburg, signed up sixty Indians, and asked them to report on the following Sunday at his farm in Palmerville. By Sunday night there were the Indians sleeping in the farm barn. They were all given a good supper and a good breakfast, and at about sunup Monday morning the whole crowd started for the woods accompanied by Uncle Juddy and Roscoe.

The caravan also included a team of horses pulling a double wagon loaded with axes, bark spuds, peaveys, saws, a cookstove, a barrel of salt pork, a barrel of white drip molasses, a barrel of flour, a couple of bales of hay and grain for the horses, and tar paper for covering the camp roofs. There was also a .38–55 Winchester rifle with enough ammunition to provide a winter supply of fresh meat off the land. This was a full load for the wagon. Dan Peck, the camp cook, joined the caravan shortly after it left Palmerville. The wagon led the way and the sixty Indians followed on foot.

At Monterey, now known as Degrasse, a stop was made to rest the horses. The Indians stopped at the tavern and got some "lung protector," which they reduced about 50 per cent at a spring further on. This mixture added walking energy to their progress and happiness to their inner selves.

At Clifton they stopped again for rest and for a meal, which they ate near the old log hotel opposite beautiful Clifton Falls and close to the old iron furnace built in 1866. Continuing along the dirt road through the woods for some twelve miles, they reached the Windfall late in the afternoon. They pulled up at Cook's for the night, ready to turn in after walking twenty-five miles since breakfast. There was plenty of liquor at Cook's, and the Indians took full advantage of this golden opportunity. Roscoe had his first encounter with bedbugs here and woke up with a riddled skin.

After breakfast the caravan continued on its way. The Indians had purchased more lung protector and now carried the bottles in bran sacks slung over their shoulders. There were many war whoops as they went along, much to Roscoe's delight. Turning onto the Windfall road, they went about a mile toward the Canton Lumber Company farm and then took off northeast on an abandoned log road, which they cleared of fallen trees. After about two miles of this they arrived at the South Branch of the Grass River near the outlet of Brother Ponds. Here they found a shallow place where the horses could wade across. Most of the Indians swam across. Uncle Juddy dropped a tall tree across the river to make the crossing easier. The caravan then followed up the outlet of Brother Ponds for a quarter mile and made camp for the night. It wasn't much of a camp, for it consisted mostly of a big fire and a place to sleep rolled up in blankets under a swarm of black flies, which were bad that June.

The next day Uncle Juddy took charge of the building operations, and soon he had large trees falling under the ax blows of the Indians. The logs were cut to the proper lengths, notched, and put in place for a sturdy log camp. The main building, some forty feet square, served as sleeping quarters for the Indians. A smaller wing was built on for cooking and eating, with two bunks at the far end for Uncle Juddy and Roscoe. Dan Peck, the cook, slept close to the stove. No doors or windows were needed in a summer logging camp like this. The white drip molasses or sorghum used on bread attracted large wasps, but they didn't sting anyone. Bears were heard on the garbage dump out back nearly every night. The black flies were a real nuisance, and one of the first things Dan Peck did was to fry out a generous supply of pork grease which Uncle Juddy mixed with a can of tar. This mixture was applied to all exposed surfaces of the skin and repelled the flies so that they didn't bother too much.

The first step in logging was to cut and peel the bark from hemlock trees. A four-foot band of bark was stripped from the base of each tree, which was then notched with an ax for direction and felled with a crosscut saw. Then a couple of Indians limbed the tree and at four-foot intervals cut through the bark around the trunk. They spudded the bark off, left it to dry for a day or two, and then heaped it into piles ready to be hauled to the tannery or the railroad. When the peeling season was over in the latter part of July, the Indians sawed the trees into logs and drew them to the skidways.

On Saturday afternoons many of the Indians headed for Cook's on the Windfall and returned late in the afternoon with a plentiful supply of lung protector, which soon stimulated considerable activity. Roscoe's description of the Indians' mixture follows: "It was concocted of one keg of whiskey, six kegs of water, and a good portion of hot pepper. When you held a glassful to the light you could see the pepper in it. I never sampled the brew myself, but they said it was real hot and stirred up those who did." There was the current belief that if the ashes from a cigar were flipped into a glass of this beverage, it knocked the drinker out cold. Uncle Juddy paid off his help in written orders signed by him, a private system of checks. Two-thirds of the vouchers went through the two taverns on the Windfall and were brought back to him to forward to Clark and Squires in Canton, where a bank check was issued to the holder.

The Hardwood Mill

Roscoe used to sit on a log by the fire and watch the Indians stirred to gaiety by the brew. They circled the fire, some dancing, some leaping and yelling. Most of them joined in a powwow dance, shouting "Ya-ho, ya-ho, ya-ha, ya-ha." After a while they became exhausted and dropped out one by one to sleep off the effects. Monday morning they were back on the job, splendid workmen and veterans in the woods.

After the first year, when these Indians from Hogansburg were used as lumber hands, French Canadian help was brought in from Canada. A Frenchman and his wife did the cooking in the camp west of Wilson Mountain, and one of the men got fresh with the wife. The cook shot and killed him with a .22 rifle. The cook and his wife came at once to my father's office in Canton, where my mother saw them. She said the Frenchwoman was a very nice, pleasant person. The cook told Father he had not thought the .22 would kill anyone. He was tried and finally released on the grounds of self-defense.

One day in the latter part of August, Roscoe saw my father come into the lumber camp and heard him report that Clark and Squires had purchased the Pearly Waite Hardwood Mill on the Oswegatchie and had also acquired from the Newton Falls Paper Company rights to cut and make into lumber the softwood down to eight inches at the stump and all the hardwood on the tract of five thousand acres lying between Newton Falls and the mill, mostly on the southwest bank of the river and including Buck Mountain. Softwood under eight inches went as pulp to the paper mill. Father said that Uncle Juddy would act as manager of the operations at the Hardwood Mill and of lumbering on the Grass River tract.

In September Roscoe's mother appeared on the scene, dragged him away from his Indian friends, and sent him to Canton to school. The following March he left Canton to join his mother at the farm in Palmerville, and from there they drove to the mill, where she took the position of chief cook for the next six years. Weekdays she had an average crew of fifty to feed, but on Sundays the number sometimes jumped to more than a hundred as many more men came in from outlying camps. There were about two hundred working in the woods and at the mill and about twenty teams in the winter drawing logs from the Grass River tract to the mill and lumber to the railroad at Newton Falls. Church services were held at the mill every Sunday, and there was a public school for the mill children, taught by Miss Rose Mosher from Crogan and Miss Edna Clark from Russell.

Cranberry Lake was our chief point of interest, and on special occasions we would harness up a team and drive to the lake. One time Roscoe and I borrowed our fathers' packbaskets, filled them up with a tent, blankets, fishing equipment, food, and a .22 rifle, and walked up to the foot of the lake. We had dinner at Bishop's White Birch Inn [operated by Bishop as an annex to the Cranberry Lake Inn]. The waitress was someone I knew from down Russell way. We were seated at long family tables when she came to take our order. Instead of giving us a menu, she started a chatter like a tobacco auctioneer, reciting the entire list from soup to nuts in such a rapid fashion that when she reached the end I could remember nothing she had said. So I told her simply, "Mary, bring on what you have."

After dinner we rented one of Rushton's Indian Girl canoes and paddled up the lake to Birch Island, where we made camp for the night. The next morning after a good breakfast of pancakes, bacon, and coffee, we started out again and paddled across to Brandy Brook. There was a heavy wind directly ahead, and the waves were so high we did not dare try to turn around. We were happy when we finally got to Barney Burns's old camp. It was a log cabin with bunks and a crude table. I do not know how long it had been out of use, but the doors were open and there was no sign of its being occupied. The table was all gnawed away by hedgehogs. We stayed there overnight and the next day returned to the mill.

There was a forest fire that nearly wiped out the Hardwood Mill, but the date escapes me. It may have been in 1908, the year of other big fires, when the remark was going around that perhaps some of the fires were set so that men could be paid for putting them out. The spring had been very dry for many weeks, and the woods were like tinder. A section from Newton Falls to the Hardwood Mill had recently been lumbered, and softwood treetops were scattered all through the area. The fire started just out of Newton Falls. Fanned by a strong wind, it became a roaring inferno. The mill stood right in the path of the fire. Uncle Juddy moved most of the records and other valuable material by speeding teams to the Windfall. Most of the population left. The yards were stacked with inflammable lumber and the whole place seemed doomed. Aunt Julia Backus refused to leave and put her trust in prayer. In five hours the fire swept the five miles from Newton Falls over Buck Mountain to within an eighth of a mile of the mill. Night had come on and the flames were belching over Buck Mountain and spreading burning leaves and bright sparks all over the place. Suddenly out of the heavens came a downpour of drenching rain. It came down for just half an hour, but when it stopped the fire had stopped too, and the Hardwood Mill was saved. This happened to be the only rain for several

The Hardwood Mill

weeks before and after the fire. Perhaps Aunt Julia's prayers were effective. I do not know.

We had a cow at the mill for milk. One late afternoon, when Uncle Juddy was coming over Buck Mountain about two miles away, he heard Roscoe calling through a four-foot handmade megaphone, "Come Boss, come Boss." Half an hour later faithful old Boss arrived at the mill, received her reward of grain for her supper, and gave us her milk. During fly season she would deposit herself close to the smudges, chewing her cud and settling down for the night. One summer a doe came to lie down on the other side of the smoking fire every night, and the next year she brought a fawn with her to the night lodging.

We had a family camp two and a half miles downstream from the steel bridge where the old Windfall road crossed the

CYRIL
BACKUS
CLARK

The Clark Family Camp, about 1912
The camp was situated on the Grass River, two miles north of the Windfall. In "miles of surrounding forest . . . the only mark of civilization." (Photo by Cyril B. Clark)

Mrs. Cyrus Clark and Miss Edna Clark

The ladies are perched atop a load of logs on the Grass River tract of Clark and Squires in 1909. Miss Edna Clark was, at this time, teaching school for the children at the lumber camp. (Photo by William Pool)

Grass River. When Father built our cottage there in 1906, the rafters, siding, clapboards, shingles, and other lumber came from the Hardwood Mill, but the main timbers were long, slim balsam trees peeled and hewn to proper shape. The lumber was drawn by team across the Windfall to a point just below the bridge, near MacAleese's. We built a boathouse here for a rowboat and a Rushton canoe. The lumber was floated down the river and hauled out at the site of the cottage.

It was a surprise to a stranger coming down the river by boat to round a bend and see a two-storied clapboard house with a big front porch and sloping lawn. In the miles of surrounding forest, it was the only mark of civilization to be seen. There were an adjoining tennis court, a croquet ground, and stakes for horseshoes, a game at which Father always beat us boys.

When we came to camp, we left our horses at MacAleese's on the hill and went by boat the rest of the way. There were three small rapids between the bridge and our camp, and we had to portage our supplies around all three. About halfway down we passed Bromley Brook with its big shelving rock by an excellent fishing hole. Our camp was just above Twin Ponds Outlet.

When the Grass River tract was sold to the Emporium Forestry Company sometime after 1910, ten acres were reserved on the river around the cottage, together with the right to hunt and fish on the entire tract. The cottage is still used as a hunting and fishing lodge.

The Hardwood Mill was sold to the Webster Lumber Company after eight years of operation by Clark and Squires. In 1910 I spent a week with friends at Bishop's White Birch Inn and drove down to take a look at the old mill property. The buildings were in good condition, but the mill was no longer running and no one was living there. Around 1930 I visited the old mill site again. The road in from the main road was then only a trail, and the bridge and most of the dam had disappeared. All the buildings were gone, and the whole place had pretty much gone back to woods.

CHAPTER IX

Warren Guinup, Lumber Jobber

Edited by ALBERT FOWLER

WARREN GUINUP was a jobber during the years of big lumbering at Cranberry Lake. He was born in 1876, learned to use an ax on his father's wood lot near Fine, and took up lumbering as a livelihood at Cranberry before the turn of the century. He logged for Clark and Squires on the Hardwood Mill lands, for Proulx and Bushie, and later for the International Paper Company. He had ingenuity and an ability to manage men. During World War I when he was logging on Six Mile Creek, he formed a fast friendship with Floyd and Jessie Oxner. Their son Ross became his bookkeeper and totemaster. In his last years Warren lived with Ross Oxner near the shore of Lake Ontario in the little town of Texas. It was here that their old friend Hugh Flick joined them on June 23, 1962, to talk about the early days at Cranberry. Hugh Flick and his family had come to the lake about the end of World War I and soon after bought the Niles cottage. For many years he counted on Warren's help and advice in the matter of docks, boats, engines, plumbing, and other intricate problems of life in the Adirondacks.

The conversation among these three men, unrehearsed and unorganized, was recorded on tape and forms the account which follows. It is through Warren's eyes that we see his early life and his later logging experiences, and it is through Ross's eyes that we examine the methods of building and managing the lumber roads, supplying the lumber camps, and keeping the lumbermen fit. Warren dominates the first half of the record and Ross the second, and Hugh Flick is always there to ask the right question and keep the story moving. No attempt has been made to separate the various voices. They are all collaborating to tell Warren's story as a lumber jobber. Warren himself, full of years and wisdom, died a few months after this conversation was recorded.

WARREN
GUINUP,
ROSS OXNER,
HUGH FLICK

My father told me there was a terrific blizzard the night I was born. It was New Year's Eve and he had to send a team of oxen to Fine to fetch the doctor. Father owned a small farm, and he did some logging off and on. Hemlock bark that come out of Clifton used to come right down across Father's old farm when I was a boy, and the road turned off this side of Fine and come right across the farm and out through into Harrisville. And I used to have a little pair of calves, this year's calves, you know. I'd break them in the winter, and I had a little hand sleigh. I'd go up and down the road and pick up pieces of bark, odds and ends. I had a lot of fun.

George Titus had a job on the farm for a while. He wanted

Lumberyards in Cranberry Lake Village, about 1922
This switching yard is the terminus of the Grass River Railroad. Cranberry Lake may be glimpsed at upper right, and Silver Pond lies to the left. (Courtesy Mrs. Clara McKenney)

Warren Guinup

For years, Guinup's lumber camp was located a short distance above Sliding Rock Falls. Guinup knew how to handle men in the woods, and he knew the ways of the forest. (Courtesy Ross Oxner)

to cut off a second cut of hemlock in little parts. He said, "That'll do you good to go down there and cut that off for us." Well, I hired some of the boys around home there and we cut the hemlocks, and he gave me the bark if I wanted to save it. Father was pretty old, but he said, "I'll go pick up the bark for you." So we cut it and skidded it up. Then we had to draw it [the lumber] way over to Jones Corners, up toward Fine.

There were a couple of big farms there. All the Jones boys owned that big farming section. I had to go over the mountain overland alone to put it in the river. I got it in, saved my bark, drawed my bark to Harrisville. When I got through I had four hundred dollars, by gosh. That's clear money.

George Titus went into the lumber business up toward Newton Falls, and he gradually worked me into it. I just got nudged into it, you know. So George had a big job up in back of that mill on the Oswegatchie, way over in there. Well, way up in there he took a big contract. He said to me, "If you're so anxious to lumber, come on up and I'll let you have a job."

WARREN
GUINUP,
ROSS OXNER,
HUGH FLICK

So I picked up an old pair of horses from the feed mill man over at Fine. He had a pair of horses and he sold me the pair. I moved up there and built a little log plant right at the foot of a big swamp. I run about twenty-five men on that little job. When we got done that year, we brought the stuff over to Newton Falls.

Then the next year he said, "Time to take another job." So I took another job up in there, and I run about twenty-five men, I guess. I helped him, you know, and he'd be working out toward Newton Falls where it was better going and I'd be picking up the back end. We worked along and when we were finished up we were pretty well up to Newton Falls, down near where that paper mill is. That cleaned him up in there too. We both cleaned up together.

That was old George Titus. He said, "Well, we've got to go to Cranberry Lake. Got wood up there. There's the Barber Tract up there." They wanted it lumbered and wanted him to come up and look it over. So him and I and my cousin, tall fellow been bossing for Titus for a while, we struck up there the night before 1903 came in. We stayed at old man Cook's, and he gave us a good bed. So George said, "Now you boys go down to the Hardwood Mill and take that line and follow it through as far as the Barber Tract." [The largest part of Barber's holdings included Glasby, Bassout, and Cat Mountain ponds, with smaller sections at the Forestry Camp and Bear Mountain.]

So we struck out with sandwiches and followed that line through and then we cut in—kept cutting in and coming back out and getting an idea of how much it was to cut per acre, you know. It was guesswork, but anybody'd been in the woods as long as I had then, I had a pretty good idea.

When we come out we were over up in Castor Creek near Wanakena, just away from Olmstead, and then we turned and came down the lake. We didn't know where we was. We knew it was Cranberry Lake, but we didn't know whether we was high or low. When we started down the shore we kept cutting into the timber and came out at old Mrs. Westcott's near the dam. It was getting pretty late and she gave us some sandwiches and then we had to walk to the Windfall, where we stayed all night and gave in a report to Titus on what we'd found and what it looked like.

Warren Guinup,
Lumber Jobber

He said, "I'll tell them I'll take the contract." So we come back down home. He said, "We'll get ready and we'll have to go back there and build some camps." So we went back and I built a camp right across from the Old Forge [on the Oswegatchie above Cook's Corners]. The old bridge had gone out, so him and I had to put in a bridge there before we could move in. We cut out an old wood road before we could really move in, you know. He went above me towards the mines and built over on a little cold brook there, and I built just across the river from the dam, almost in sight of the dam.

I must have had about twenty-five men, and we had to put up camps and barns and everything. Then when I got it going we had to peel it all [the spruce], and I finished up that job that year. I peeled all that I had agreed to peel. And a fellow by the name of Chadwick from out down in Pitcairn come up and took the job with George above me toward Benson Mines. He didn't make a go of it. So the next year I had to pick up his job and come back toward the Hardwood Mill. So I went down to the Hardwood Mill and started a big camp there that held fifty men.

And this man Titus wasn't over in this camp long before he died. They wouldn't give me, the company wouldn't give me the whole tract of lumber, see. They thought I was too young. They thought maybe I wouldn't make a go of it. So they give it to a man named Proulx from Tupper Lake. So Proulx moved in and took Titus's side to finish up, and that went clean out to the state land where we come up across from Benson Mines. I was two years down in that camp. But during the two years that I was cleaning out the pulp, the Hardwood Mill had a new outfit move in there. Sold to a different lumber outfit. And they wanted me to pick up hardwood. They wanted me to pick that up for them on the same tract. That's why I had so many men finishing up the spruce, so as to take care of the hardwood.

Warren Guinup, Ross Oxner, Hugh Flick

That was much heavier to handle. You had to have good horses, and then you had to have a lot of sawing. And you had to have good men to know their business. I cleaned it all up the second year we were down there. As soon as we got through that job—put the hardwood down and got the spruce all out—the fellows that had the hardwood, they just felt they were broke and they couldn't pay me at all. But they let me have some lumber to build camps. Whatever I wanted to take, I could take.

So I went up there to Frank Wilder's old place and built a camp below him. I built a camp up in there in the edge of the bay. I used their lumber, took that up there to build my camp. So that was all I got out of that. But we built a good set of camps there to hold fifty men, and we lumbered all that section clean back to the line that we first went over, clean up to Tramps Retreat.

Well, I managed to make something every year, you know, enough to keep going. So when I got that all lumbered—I can't remember whether I was two or three years before I got up across the lake—I cut pulp up on the mountain, Round Top, right there at the head of West Flow. You remember that little island or kind of island when you went into West Flow? There was an old lumber camp that had been in there years ago. Well, I went into these old camps that they had over there. That was so that I could draw that, and gosh I had got a good start drawing, but we had quite a lot of hemlock in with the spruce. When we got it loaded on skids, we had to have calked skids, skids with spikes, or they would slip on us. They'd be so big we couldn't handle them.

So this Sunday morning, it was the first of December, I said, "I'll make some calked skids so we'll have them for next week." I went out back. My brother was blacksmithing for me, and my cousin was working for me. I went out and I cut a skid about twelve foot long and six inches through. I had it on my shoulder and went along, and just as I turned to go up to the blacksmith shop I stepped on the edge of a stone. A sleigh had hit it and made it icy, you know, and gee, my feet went out from under me, my head went right down and hit that stone right there—got the mark of it still—and the skid went right across my head. The boys down in the men's camp had been watching me and seen me fall. They come and picked me up. My nephew was working for me, too—choreboy. So they come and picked me up. Oh, God, I was knocked right out. I didn't know nothing.

*Warren Guinup,
Lumber Jobber*

Well, they knew I'd want the doctor, so they rode me out on a log sleigh—put some plank on it and took me down to the foot of the lake. Old Mike Brainerd was there. Old Mike, he was going to be good to me, and he gave me a drink of liquor and that made me bleed all the worse. They had to get a pair of horses from Newton Falls to come up and pick me up, and they took me down to the hospital. I was in the hospital from December to March.

I wanted the doctor to operate on me, you know. He said, "Not there." He said, "We ain't going to take any more chances with pulling you through than you've got right now." So anyway I was in the hospital till March. When I got home they all had to lead me around. Somebody had to take my hand. I couldn't see where I was stepping. It was a month or two before I could see to walk, but it kept getting better all the while.

They kept right on lumbering while I was in the hospital, and then I went right on up Six Mile Creek. Kept going up, and I lumbered all that section as the years went by. I guess it was a couple of years before I built them big camps up to Sliding Rock. We didn't branch out again until I went way up to a little pond just this side of Wolf Mountain, I think it was. I had a big camp up there, and I finished up in there. A fellow by the name of Noonan now has a camp up in there.

When I got through and was back there hunting, a fellow

came in there one morning. He said, "I've been looking for you." I said, "What the darn do you want?" He said, "I want you to go over to Tug Hill. I've got a big steam skidder over there and it is on the railroad tracks and I can't skid logs with it. If there is a man that could make that thing skid logs, I'm going to find him. And I came right up here to see if you would go over to Tug Hill." So I went over to Tug Hill [the high plateau west of Boonville].

Here they had these two big cars, electric light outfit, you know, for power and light. And these big log cables that went way back up there on the top of the hill. And a revolving drum up there with the cables on it. They call it a lumberman's leg or a moosecat. These cables went back in the woods, and you hook several logs to one end and then you draw them out to a skidway. The fellow running the outfit thought he knew all about it, and what he done when he set it up was to cut just one line through and come right back with the same cable. So when it came out it had the logs and when it went back it had the grapples, and when they came together they'd stick the whole thing. He had to take a pair of horses and go out there and pull them apart, and that's when he come up to Cranberry and had me go over.

"Now," he said, "what would you do if you were doing it? I'm going to get the hell out of here until it's done, and I know it's going to be done, too." So he said, "It's all yours," and went out of his office. So I went and looked it over. I went back to the office, called up Mel, and told him I'd got to have some more cable. I said, "You can't do anything in here unless you put a reel-haul in back, something to handle that cable." "Well," he said, "you shall have some right out. We'll send some right up." So up it comes, so I put a reel-haul in back, put some more blocks in, a block here and a block over there, and it didn't take long to fix that.

But the man that was running the engine, Jack, couldn't see what was going on back in the woods, so the fellow back hooking the logs, he had a whistle and he blew that and the next fellow could hear him and he'd blow a whistle. They would blow several times for the man that was at the steam controls. Well, they didn't always get their whistles working right, and the logs were going when they hadn't ought to and it was quite a control system. Jack didn't know whether to stop and go back or go ahead. Well, I had to walk the whole length to tell them what to do. That's how I got the telephones. Then I just had to step up to this little plant and call Jack, and Jack would know just what to do, back up or go ahead.

Higbee, he came on one day and he said, "How are you coming?" "Well," I said, "I'd be coming a lot faster if I had some batteries to work this telephone line I've got up here. They get me a half dozen of these little batteries, you know, six-inch batteries that won't last over fifteen minutes. Them little batteries don't last as long as I take to put them in there." "Well," he said, "I'll have a battery up here." So he went right out and got a handcar and had one of the men take him down, and he got a battery and came right back with it. "Now," he said, "let's see you skid logs." "When I get this thing straightened out you'll see some logs," I said. When I got it lined up he stayed there and he seemed scared, you know. Hell, I was sending logs down to the mill hell bent for leather. He said, "I told you if there was a man in this country who could make that thing work I was going to get him. Well, sir, you certainly know how to handle the woods." And I stayed on at Tug Hill till I cleaned it all up.

They were big logs, big birch, you know. Some of them we'd have to put them on a kind of stone boat. But as a rule the men would just nose them a little and then the grabs would drive the end and keep them lifted up, and if a log got to dipping in a hole, why, I had men just skid that with the small stuff. Then we worked down to the branch of the road and went across Tug Hill over by Boonville.

Higbee, he put the skidder over on the other line. He wanted to be cheap and he hired an old man, like myself now, who couldn't hardly get around, you know, to watch at nights.

Warren Guinup, Lumber Jobber

Warren
Guinup,
Ross Oxner,
Hugh Flick

There was a big gas tank, and they didn't want a lot of fire around. But the old man, he got in there this night and he must have got cold, and he built a fire right out a little ways from the gas tank. Well, all of a sudden he come up to my room up at the Y and woke me up. I had to go and get the boss and wake him up, and then I had to wake everybody and go fight fires.

That whole damn thing was burning right up. Oh, boy! The big car that run the drums, we did manage to save that. Then when we got it all cleaned up again and started to go, I said, "Aren't you going to get some more rope for this thing?" "Well," he said, "I'm going to use that same thing we pulled off there." "That'll be burnt," I said. "That rubber, the inside of that'll be burnt right out." "No," he said, "that'll be all right, we'll use that. I ain't going to spend more money." We put it on and it broke first thing. So he had to go to work and buy whole new cable. But I stayed there until it was all cleaned up.

When they brought in the skid method to Cranberry, it was a Pennsylvania idea with the logs in a trough and a team of horses straddling it. A party by the name of Smith was the first to bring it in over there at Carter's Crossing. They made a kind of trough and covered the inside of it with some kind of black grease they had, and the logs were rolled into this. They would have maybe fifty or sixty logs. Then a team of horses straddled this as they went in the back end with a grab hook drove in the last log, and it pushed that whole business in the greasy trough.

The logs would average from ten to twelve feet, fifty logs probably. Well, that went all right until they went over a little raise in the ground and the logs started going down on their own. The first log stuck and the second piled up on it, and then they all jumped the trough after that, and then they had to reload it again.

George Bushie, he tried to make a trough up on Indian Mountain and drove over into South Flow where the falls is, and he was going to straddle it and put the logs in and let it slide. It got piled up and all messed up. So he gave it up after a while, and he left all the lower side of the mountain. He didn't put it in on his job. And they got me to go over and clean it up. On all the lower side we just crowned out a sleigh road, you know, and sanded the hills, and I cleaned it up and that was my way of doing it.

They had a big slide off of the mountain, and they made it come down and had built an abutment—had it way up in the air—and those logs would come down there, and when they would jump off'n there they would pile up. It cost a lot of money to build the abutment up that high, over one hundred feet high. Well, it worked, but there was a limited amount of lumber that could be got off'n there. It was not successful due to the fact that these logs were dropping over one hundred feet,

Warren Guinup,
Lumber Jobber

Log Chute off Indian Mountain, 1915
Logs were hauled to the upper end of the chute by horses and slid over the cliff down to South Flow. (Photo by Fay Welch)

and it shattered them. When they would hit, a lot of them would break. What didn't break would be drove halfway down in the mud in the bottom of the flow, and probably some of them are down in there yet. Well, it was torn down, but it was still there around 1918, 1920, 1924, in back of the Indian Mountain Hotel. And then Bill Mott, he dynamited the chute and dropped it down, and the logs were in a good state of preservation up there, so he cut it up for firewood.

I just got through cleaning up over at Tug Hill, and old man Hostler of Long Lake, he came over and said, "Young Biddle died last night." He was doing that job for him out around Little Trout Farm up by Bog River. He said, "I haven't got nobody that can boss for me. I want you to go over and help me out." So I took over Little Trout Farm, and my nephew went with me to cook. So I finished up that job, and I kept right on going until I went right through to Bog River. Before I got through I was lumbering up at Long Lake. That was softwood.

For all the years I lumbered, I can say one thing. I never was fired. You can change cooks. You can change blacksmiths. And you can change bosses if you feel like it. But I never was fired yet. I'd take the contract, and the company furnished the money, so much for me, and I'd give my payroll in, and they'd see that I had the money. But I never had to make out a payroll. International Paper Company's Wilbur, he said, "By God, if I can't trust you enough to pay those men, what in hell do I want with you?" He was a rough old fellow.

When we first went into lumbering, you paid a man a dollar a day and you thought you was doing pretty good. Things would get a little bit better, a little bit better, and you paid a good man forty dollars. The good men would show up and you would give them a little bit better, and all the others would be held back. You had to go according to the men you had and what they were worth. And then I began to raise the good men that knew what to do and would do it, and instead of going and hiding someplace they would be working. There was a lot of logging done at from twenty-six to thirty dollars a month, and then as the men got better we would give them forty dollars a month.

I never had much trouble with my help. The only trouble I had was with the Russians they sent in here when I was running right up that swamp toward Olmstead Pond. It was in wartime, and they were sending in a lot of Russians along about that time. Well, they didn't know what to do, but they were big and stout. They'd have to have men with them all the while, and it was hard work to get a horse through that swamp. But you could give them some tools and they would carry a lot of that stuff right out, those young fellows. That's the way I skidded that swamp.

Then they came down to the lower camp. They swarmed on me to pay them the same amount of money I was paying the other men. I told them I couldn't do it. They said I'd either pay them more money or I'd wish I had. To that effect, you know, as near as I could understand. My little old .38 lay right behind me, so I just reached over and I picked that up and I said, "Will this argue with you a bit? Now you better get right on the road and I'll follow you right down there." I followed him right down to Pig's Ear, to the saloon. He took the money when I give him the check. Put him on the old boat. Never saw him again.

Old man Cook, who had the old hotel on the Windfall, furnished the money to build Pig's Ear Saloon there at Chair Rock, and Bill Mott ran it. He used to have nights when he would send out to get a couple of girls from Watertown. He'd have them left over at Merrill's Point. He'd send for me. I had a little boat. "Go over and get them girls." I'd go over and get the girls. Have the boys come down. They'd get drunk and he'd send them over to the house.

There was Shannon and his sleigh. He was known as Babe Shannon. He was well over six feet and quite a character in the lumber business. Well, he had this team and he sent them up there and we put a load of logs on him, and he started and

Warren Guinup,
Lumber Jobber

WARREN
GUINUP,
ROSS OXNER,
HUGH FLICK

when he got to the hill there, to the place where the sleighs break over, he was so scared that he tried to stop the darn thing. He cracked his horses around, you know, and they went right down and right over this bump and killed one horse. He jumped and saved himself. It was the first time the men had ever seen Babe Shannon scared. That really subdued him.

They had men that they called sand monkeys. They would dig a pit in the sandpile, chop the sand out, heat it in cans, and then sprinkle it on the downgrades so that actually your team drawed the load of logs downhill. If they didn't, the sleighs would gain momentum. Babe's father worked on the Sand Hill [name commonly given to the steepest hill on a long haul], and he knew just what to do to catch those fellows when they breaked over. They had to have a little stop, you know. Why, they'd be going down through like nobody's business. You couldn't stop them dead right at the top of the hill. A lot of the safety of the horses and equipment depended on the sand monkey working on that hill. Especially on a day when it was snowing or sleeting. He was a very busy person. The sand monkey where there was a bad hill was one of the most important men because you can imagine what one of those loads of logs would do if it ever got away.

Sometimes a lumber camp would get snowed in, and they would be several days plowing out the road. You see, they had to plow that road by ordinary snowplows. Sometimes they would have a plow the same as you would use in a field but with another board in back of the moldboard. And they would take one of these old iron kettles and drag that behind the plow as they were coming back, and it would make a concave surface. And then the sprinkling tank came along and worked that down and froze it. It would make a pretty hard slippery road too. That was the common practice.

How did they keep the water in the sprinkler from freezing? Well, it was a very simple thing. They would have a can, like a twenty- or thirty-gallon milk can, and they would heat it full of boiling water and dump that in the tank and then stop at the first creek and bail the tank full of water. Well, that kept it from freezing, but if it did get froze at the sprinkling head across the back they would build a fire under it. The sprinkler man, he was going maybe all night—shovel snow and pack it down and sprinkle it and build it up again. Your sanding crew would be up early in the morning to throw the sand on it. If it was real cold the sand would be frozen, and they would have to build a fire with roots and rotten logs and pine knots with pitch in them to thaw out the sand.

They used lamps at night, and you would use torches on your first load—make them out of cloth and things and stick them in the snow to start in loading in the morning. The teams would be out before it was light. Then they had the long torches that hung up with two prongs on them [as a swivel to hold an oil-burning flare] like a broom handle. They held about a quart of coal oil. I bet those have all disappeared now.

Oh, yes, there was a pile of dynamiting. It was not uncommon in the wintertime, where there was a road alongside of a stream, they would get a thaw and a little ice jam would come in the stream. It would be up to three or four feet high, and it would start flooding the road. Well, then you would send the dynamite monkey down and he would blow the jam up, and you would be back in business. If you didn't you could be tied up the rest of the winter if that froze solid. If it got up on the road and would freeze, you would have to chop up miles of that ice.

There was this fellow Ugly Mike O'Mara. Anybody would hire up Mike in a minute if they were establishing a new camp, for laying out roads. All Mike would have to do was to walk up through a piece of timber and he would say, "We'll put the haul road right through here." And he could select with his eye what it would take a trained engineer a week to do. And that was probably the difference between profit and loss, too, if you could get an Ugly Mike O'Mara and a good cook.

Most of the tote roads were built on the hills, but some went right in the swamps. Some swamps we had to corduroy. That

Warren Guinup,
Lumber Jobber

143

swamp by Sliding Falls, I had that all corduroyed and that corduroy stayed in good, too, didn't it? Stayed in for years and years. The bridge at Sliding Falls is still there. It's a good bridge.

WARREN
GUINUP,
ROSS OXNER,
HUGH FLICK

I furnished all the tools. I bought all the handsaws, all the crosscut saws and the axes, and we issued them out to the men if they wanted them. When I went to work for Hostler over there at Long Lake, he had different camps running. He was supposed to furnish that camp with axes and saws and so forth. Why, he couldn't buy them fast enough. They were just burying them. Hal Brainerd started in to boss for him. He was a young kid. Harold didn't care how much he lost or how much he made. So he let Harold go and he got me over there. I come to find out that a man took an ax out, and if it wasn't sharp or if he didn't like the heft of it or didn't like the looks of it, he'd throw it away and go in and get another one. So I just said, "Here, young man, here's your ax, your handle. If you break it accidentally, you put in a new one. If you break it on purpose, you will pay for it. And if you throw one of these saws away, or if you throw one of these axes away, you are going to pay for that unless I find out that it is no good."

We worked a lot of the men all summer, and some of them would stay on through the winter. When the logs were all piled up ready for the hauling, they would maybe take a week or two off and then they would be back for the winter work. Some would quit and some wouldn't.

They sent the pulpwood down the Oswegatchie, just let it sluice right through. That's when they had the big long sluice there at the dam. Old Herb Dean used to drive most of that down the river. He was a good boss. He knew his business. The men wouldn't follow the logs down. They generally made a deal with Dean, and he hired the help he wanted on the river.

The Emporium Forestry Company tried to take their hardwood down the lake on scows. [Hardwood logs do not float well.] They tried to put softwood in under them and they would shift any time they would have a blow. Then the next

Cranberry Lake Dam
The sluice is for floating pulpwood down the Oswegatchie. (Courtesy John Aldrich)

thing was they bored three-inch holes in the end of the logs and plugged them to cut off the air space. They'd float so low in the water that they would jump the boom. Ross, one of the first jobs your father had up there was in a little boat going around towing in those old logs that were floating about two feet under water. You know, they're still pulling those logs out of the lake up there now, and getting $110 a thousand for them down at the foot of the lake, for just logs.

My experience in peeling bark was all spruce. We peeled spruce, you know. Saved loss in handling. Spruce was easier to handle peeled, lighter to handle. It dried out. You wouldn't use the bark. You'd just throw that away. That was quite a trick, peeling spruce. Had to have a good spudder. That was a long blade, about a foot long. It had a kind of knife on it. You could have it sharp if you wanted it.

With hemlock the head spudder would ring the tree every four feet, about. The fitters would chop in so the fellow with

WARREN
GUINUP,
ROSS OXNER,
HUGH FLICK

the spud could break the bark off—spud it off. It'd come off in sheets. You could take as big sheets as you wanted to. Years and years ago they just used the bark [in tanning leather], and the trees would lay there and rot unless somebody picked them up. Then they come to use the lumber mostly, and the bark rotted away. The bark was shipped to some tannery, and pretty soon a man didn't get enough out of it to hardly pay the freight on it. The last bark shipped out of Cranberry Lake was in 1916. I had cut and piled it at the siding at the foot of the lake, and Fred Brunswick and Ross [Oxner] loaded those two carloads that went out of there. Ross was eighteen years old and had no idea of bark, and it was a great curiosity to him what they were going to do with that bark. And that same year, 1916, Hugh [Flick] went to the lake the first time, and when he went to the Forestry Camp that whole bluff there was gray with this huge pile of hemlock bark. It just rotted away. No one ever moved it.

What would the men in the camps do for recreation at night? Well, the boys would have a place over in the woods

"Heading for the mill . . ."
A float of logs is towed down Cranberry Lake. (Courtesy John Aldrich)

where they would go and play poker. They would not let them play in the camp, so they would go over there and play. If you had a bunch of jobbers and the men working for them, they would find a place to play one way or another.

Warren Guinup,
Lumber Jobber

I was telling Ross about Starkey's brother, Joe Starkey. He was running one of the camps. He was to come up this Sunday morning with the payroll. (I had the payroll made up in the office, and always on Sunday he would bring it up.) But this day he didn't come and didn't come and we thought he had passed it over or something, but the next morning some of the men came up and said, "Have you seen Starkey?" And we said, "No, we ain't seen Starkey," and finally there was nobody to open up the camp. We couldn't find Starkey and we never did find him. He just disappeared and never even picked up his pay check.

Ross wants me to explain how they would keep clean in the camps and how they would have an old copper kettle out there to boil their clothes in and get the body lice off and the bedbugs. Well, there was a big black kettle there, and two or three would get together and build a fire and get some water and boil their clothes. And then another bunch would come and wash their clothes. They'd do this every weekend.

He wants me to explain why there were always bedbugs in the lumber camps. They were in the basswood stumps. You can always find bedbugs right out in the woods. There were the swampers [men who cleared out brush and rotten logs]. As you were building a road, you would have a couple of swampers working ahead. And they would just get loaded with these bedbugs off of that rotten basswood in there. And they would bring bedbugs back into the lumber camp. There was a constant battle to get the camp cleaned out each week.

They had a kind of tick, too. Just the same as you find on a bat, these small red lice that a bat will always have under its wings. And the bats would bring these into the camp with them, and that is why there was always this constant battle in the camps with bedbugs and body lice and trying to get them cleaned up. They would use yellow soap, and they would have straw mattress ticks. They would shake the straw out, put the mattress ticks in water, and boil them up, then go out to the barn and stuff them full of fresh straw and spray the wooden boards in their bunks with kerosene, and they would be pretty much immune for a couple of weeks.

They used to use lard for the mosquitoes. They would take a couple of drops of roofing tar and mix it in a pound of lard. That's what they used to keep the punkies off with. Regular coal-tar lard. I've got some of it here, and it's what they used in the camps. A couple of drops of roofing tar in a pound of lard and work it up. Just smear it all over. That really gave them punkies something to think about.

If a man got hurt or got sick, there was only two things they knew to do. When I got hurt up there, the only two things they'd do was to give me money and to bring me liquor. I didn't need either one of them, but I still got it. Their real remedy that they still went by was pine pitch. If there was anything that they could get pine pitch on, pine pitch went on it. Whether it was a cut or an impacted wisdom tooth or an ingrown toenail, it got pine pitch. Strange as it may seem, nothing really ever happened from it. They never heard of an infection from it. They would go up to where there was some running out of a tree and smear it on, put a rag around it, and go on to work.

There used to be some ministers come through the camps, even those that were back in. They used to come over to Flat Rock. They would come in, generally two of them, over from Harrisville. We would feed them, let them sleep in the office, you know, and then they would go over to the men's camps, sometimes spend a couple of days. They would hold a prayer service for the men, and it wasn't uncommon to have a priest come in and spend a day or two with them. You would sometimes find Mike the Mariner, they used to call him, or Ugly Mike [O'Mara]. He would hold prayer meeting with four or five of the boys. They would go over in the cooks' camp and

Laying the Rails for the Grass River Railroad
The railroad was built by the Emporium Forestry Company in 1911–13. (Courtesy John Aldrich)

they would set down at a table and he would read Scripture with the boys and be something like a missionary and explain it to the boys. I don't know why they nicknamed the poor old man Ugly Mike. He wasn't ugly, but maybe it was because he was so religious. He was one of the best swampers that you had up in the camps for laying out roads. He could see the possibilities of a road right up over the side of a hill.

The men in the camp seemed to all have a great habit of singing. It was quite a deal of a morning, say on a frosty morn-

WARREN
GUINUP,
ROSS OXNER,
HUGH FLICK

ing when you could hear a man's voice for several miles when it was ten or fifteen below. You'd see one man coming down the skidway, and he was singing in English some popular song and right behind him there was a Frenchman and he was singing in French. It was quite a contrast to hear him jabbering. It at least showed they were happy. Whether they could sing or not, it seemed to be a custom.

They usually had a banjo player or a violin player in the camps. Many of the nights were spent in singing what we could call folk songs. There would be somebody who was a good tap dancer or did the "buck and wing" or "turkey in the straw."

Log Train of the Rich Lumber Company
The train travels the rails between Wanakena and Benson Mines. (Courtesy John Aldrich)

They made up their own songs, too, like "Ugly Mike" or "Big George of Squaw Valley." There were quite a few of them like that. Mostly they would sing the songs that were being sung at that time, and then they would have these ballads they would make up. It was not uncommon that if anyone, say, fell off a log, why, by that night they would have a ballad about him that somebody had made up.

Warren Guinup,
Lumber Jobber

The diet in the camps was something. Today a man would walk into a restaurant in New York City and would have to pay six or seven bucks to get a meal like they served in the camps. White bread, brown bread, pies, and when they would have ham they didn't serve just one piece of ham, they had a big platter of ham. After the first round the boy that was taking care of the tables filled them up again. The pies went along right on the table. If you didn't feed them well, they moved off to find a camp that fed better.

We had to carry in all our stoves and all that equipment. Everything that was in the camp had to be lugged in. You had usually a team and a man that did the toting. All their job was to keep supplies coming into the camp. If the trail was mostly rock so you couldn't use a wagon, which it usually was, you had a sleigh or the forward two wheels of a wagon and two trailing poles dragging in back with a box on them. Every day they would go down to the landing wherever the boats landed, if it was that type of a camp, and they would bring their supplies up. Ed Latray and Ross did the toting for me for one year with a boat, and they could bring in the hay and grain and groceries and roofing paper, even the clothing—everything that you wanted.

In the camps we always had a little store in the office. When many of the men came in to work they were not too well clothed, so we would have shirts and stockings and underwear and the things a man would wear—shoes, boots—and a calk driver to drive calks in their shoes for them. Driving logs, they had to have shoes with calks in them or they would break their necks. They were spikes, yes, calks we called them.

WARREN
GUINUP,
ROSS OXNER,
HUGH FLICK

In the wintertime we'd do the same thing across the ice. We would drive down. That would be a long cold ride across a lake like Cranberry. We'd go every day. You see, we had the teams in there, and how much hay and grain would they need in a day? A man would bring a load of hay and grain, and groceries piled up. To serve ham to a crew like that you would have six or seven hams, with three big copper boilers on the stove just boiling ham. The beef would come in frozen—chunk beef, frozen solid.

How did they keep food in a lumber camp in the summer? If you found a spring, you built a springhouse over it. It worked on the principle of these water pipes you use in India with condensation keeping them cold. You built one log building and you put another one around it and filled that with about a foot of dirt in between. Then you had shelves in this building with this stream flowing just in under them in a double building. It would keep as cool as in an icehouse with the condensation off that creek. You would have your shelves in there for your butter and everything. The only thing that would happen was that you would have a mink or a coon and he would find that he could swim in the creek and come up into the stockroom. He would have a ball for himself. About the worst animal you could get would be a coon. You really had a house inside a house, yes, with dirt in between. You would find it in all camps. Sometimes they would have a spring, and a spring did not seem to work as good as a little running brook.

Horses were one of your biggest problems as consumers of food. And you would have to keep them in shoes. In the wintertime you had to have winter shoes. For that you would have a blacksmith right in the camp, and that was all he did.

There was a great deal of rivalry among the drivers with regard to ornaments on the horses and the care of the horses. The first thing in the morning they had to see how the horses had slept through the night, and at night they had to put them to bed. You had a large stable and regular warm closed stalls. They would have a great rivalry as to which man had the best-looking team. I don't know that I ever saw a poor horse or one that looked underfed in a lumber camp. The horses got to be almost as expert as the drivers did. They knew exactly where to step and how to step and how to keep away from ice.

There was an old superstition that may have been true that there weren't any snakes in the Adirondacks originally, and that all the snakes came in with the bales of hay that were brought up. Now there is quite a large snake population, and it all came maybe from the lumber camps.

You would have men of all ages in the camps. It was not uncommon to have men seventy years old, down to a chore boy of maybe twelve years old. Many of them had families back home. They would be off up in the woods away from home, and that's why it seems to me they had a quality that you don't find today. If a man would come in and his little girl was sick and had to go to the hospital and he didn't have enough money, they wouldn't even think about getting an advance. I never heard of anyplace where they were that free with their money. They would all chip in to get him money for an operation. They seemed to have this code among themselves that you wouldn't find in the outside world. The first thing was a donation if anybody was hurt or sick or needed money for some misfortune at home, his wife was sick or something. They would do that of themselves. You didn't have to go and collect it from them.

Warren Guinup,
Lumber Jobber

153

CHAPTER X

The Making of a Woodsman

FAY WELCH

FAY WELCH has seen Cranberry Lake through the eyes of cottager, guide, naturalist, forestry student and teacher, and conservationist. When he first came to the lake in 1903, he brought with him the eager eyesight and mindsight of boyhood. The lake and its surroundings have not only kept those qualities alive and fresh, deepened and refined them, but have also influenced his choice of careers.

After graduation from the State College of Forestry at Syracuse, he became a teacher there and an authority on forest recreation. He has served as camp counselor, director, and consultant and is the author of more than a hundred articles and booklets on camping, skiing, hiking, winter mountaineering, and other outdoor activities; also on conservation in general and New York State's Forest Preserve in particular. He has served as chairman of the Advisory Committee on Camping of the National Park Service and as a director of the National Audubon Society. He represents Madison County on the New York State Conservation Council. As a former governor of the Adirondack Mountain Club and currently as a trustee of the Association for the Protection of the Adirondacks, he has done everything in his power to keep the Adirondacks "forever wild."

In a speech at the annual meeting of the Adirondack Mountain Club in Albany in 1954, Fay Welch remarked that trying to put into words the inspiration given by the "remnants of primeval forest, by the uncut wooded lake shores, by the autumn colors or the mountaintop views is like trying to put into print the emotions aroused by a great cathedral or a splendid symphony." In the following recollections—aided by his own diaries and journals and by those of his mother and his uncle, Thomas W. Hamer—he does attempt to put in words the inspiration he received from Cranberry Lake in early years. The woods and waters were his best teachers. Cranberry has been many things to many men. To Fay Welch it was an education.

INITIATION

FAY WELCH

Our family first discovered Cranberry Lake in 1902 when a cousin, Ed Deremo, purchased the area later known as Deremo Point on the shore between Joe Indian Island and Indian Mountain.

The following year Ed started the construction of the Deremo Hotel, a four-story frame structure. The main timbers were hewed from tall spruces growing near the head of the first little bay beyond the point. I remember that the big chips made wonderful boats, platters, and other childhood toys. The hotel faced Bear Mountain and Brandy Brook. Broad porches extended all the way across the front of the first two stories, and there was a smaller porch above. These commanded a sweeping view of the widest portion of the lake.

In 1903 Cranberry Lake was largely a wilderness, an untouched and exceedingly beautiful area, its waters abounding in trout and its numerous bogs and impenetrable bays— blocked by standing and fallen tree trunks and driftwood—a haven for wildlife. Today it is difficult to convey to a newcomer an idea of the beauty of the primeval forest that bordered the lake and mantled the mountainsides. Many of today's bare rock ledges were then hidden under towering pines, spruces, and hemlocks.

On July 2, 1903, my grandfather, Thomas Hamer; my mother, Mina Welch; her friend, Mary Woodruff, and I made our first trip to Cranberry Lake. We traveled by train from Lacona near the eastern end of Lake Ontario to Watertown and then on to Benson Mines. There we changed to a "side-wheeler" [a Shay locomotive, with gear shaft along the outer side of the right-hand wheels] which hauled our train six miles to where the village of Wanakena was being hewed out of the wilderness. I remember that trees were being uprooted by a donkey engine from what was later the center of the little village.

With our baggage we climbed on board the *Zenda,* a small white cabin steamboat piloted by Captain Henry Mullen, who had a camp on the Narrows a mile downstream. Almost everywhere the trunks of dead trees projected from the water, interlaced with fallen logs and driftwood, relics from the flooding in '67. At the Hawk's Nest just before the Inlet opened into Dead Creek Flow, the tangle was so bad that the boat was brought to a stop with one limb almost through a window. I will never forget the picture of Captain Mullen going over the side, ax in hand, and chopping logs in two and cutting off limbs so that the boat could get through. A few years later the state appropriated money for clearing the channel.

Six Mile Creek at South Flow
This photograph was taken before logging began, when the trail from the Indian Mountain House to Sliding Rock Falls passed across the bridge. (Courtesy John Aldrich)

Another unforgettable sight was the Hopyard. This was an area on the left, north of the Howlett camp, as we neared the lake proper, where the gaunt tamarack trunks emerging from the water were so extensive and numerous that we could not see through them to the shore beyond. Most of them were cut off a winter or two later for firewood for the local hotels.

We arrived at the Deremo dock by midafternoon. Grandfather selected a tent site for us near the shore to the west between the hotel and the little bay. He helped us erect the tent and make balsam-bough beds. A few feet in front of the tent was our fireplace, with a crane. Here we spent several happy weeks, in spite of the mosquitoes.

At this time Cranberry Lake was almost completely surrounded by magnificent virgin forest. There had been a little cutting by the settlers in the vicinity of Cranberry Lake Village. Now the Rich Lumber Company was about to start operations around Wanakena. The only lumbering operation on the main part of the lake was in the vicinity of Sucker Brook. There Dunc McDonald and his four sons had set up a rossing (debarking) mill, from which they shipped four-foot pulpwood by scow to Cranberry Lake Village.

In 1904 my uncle, Fred Smart, built a cottage with the help of his brother-in-law, Thomas W. Hamer, and my father, James Welch, on a lot to the southeast of Deremo Point. He had pre-cut all the material for it—rafters, studs, floor joists, and window and door frames—at his mill in Lacona and shipped it by freight car to Wanakena. It reached the cottage site by boat in late June. The two-and-a-half-story camp of six rooms, two halls, and two large porches was completed on July 7. "Forest Home," as it was called, was to be our headquarters for many years to come and is still used by members of the family.

The year of the great fires, 1908, had been exceedingly dry. On October 12 Fayette Salisbury, my father, and I started from home for Cranberry. Up Benson Mines way, smoke filled the air, and at one place before reaching Wanakena we could see the flames licking the dead conifer tops that had been left by the lumbermen. Here and there men were fighting the fires.

The Oswegatchie River, which would usually float good-sized steamers, was nothing but a small creek in front of the dock at Wanakena. We shouldered our packs and walked down along its dried mud banks for over half a mile before we

Forest Home—Fay Welch Standing on the Dock

Since its completion, July 7, 1904, the cottage has seen continuous service as family headquarters for the Smarts, Welches, Hamers, and Widrigs, and is still in use today. (Photo by James Welch)

came to a place where it would float our rented rowboat. We traveled many extra miles on our way down to the lake, looping far up Dead Creek Flow, which now was dry almost from shore to shore with a meandering creek snaking its way down toward the lake. Joe Indian Island was now a peninsula. Later my father would walk across to it from the mainland, but now we had to row far down toward Cranberry Lake Village, around the Bear Mountain side of the island, and finally back to Forest Home.

Fires were burning in many directions. The one threatening us was burning from Cat Mountain toward Round Top Mountain, directly behind our cottage. I remember being out on the lake one night and looking at Grass Hill, which was smoking like a half-dead bonfire, with little points of light speckling its side.

Ed Deremo, who had built a little cottage about fifty yards to the west of Forest Home after his hotel burned on November 2, 1907, told us that he had been back in the woods and found that the fire had burned over Round Top Mountain and was slowly moving our way. We started clearing a fire trail from our spring, near the site of the old Witch Bay camp, to the head of the little bay to the west of the point, as this would save both cottages and some adjacent forest. This fire trail was swept clear of autumn leaves, all sticks and branches were removed, and containers with water were placed at intervals along it. Men from the Indian Mountain House were building a similar protective trail around the Merrill (now Cole) and the Niles (now Flick) cottages.

Fayette Salisbury had to return home on October 20, and much to my disgust my dad decreed that because of the mounting forest fire danger I must accompany him. Now we were able to get a rowboat only to the Livingston Spring Hole, a short distance below the present Ranger School. From there we walked to Wanakena.

The fire trails, supplemented by the efforts of several fire fighters, saved the four cottages, but the point between Forest

Home and the Merrill cottage, which at that time was covered with a magnificent growth of stately hemlocks and spruces, was completely ruined. Much of the soil, even, was burned away, as it was largely composed of duff, the accumulation of decayed tree trunks and leaves over hundreds of years. What had been a deep carpet, absorbing moisture like a great sponge and giving it out slowly, was suddenly changed into a boulder-strewn graveyard. Soil specialists estimate the topsoil thus destroyed may have been five thousand years in building up.

Trout fishing was still good around Cranberry Lake in the second decade of the century. All the fish caught were brook trout (*Salvelinus fontinalis*). Size was seldom recorded, except for the larger ones of two pounds or more. From the lake a "good" or "nice" trout referred to one around twelve inches long or larger. We usually returned trout to the lake that were under nine inches, but kept all legal ones (over six inches) taken in the ponds. The daily limit at that time was ten pounds per person.

Of all the trout that I caught during these years, I remember only one as an individual. His portrait, in oil, is before me as I write. His length was fifteen and a half inches, his depth three and a half, and his weight approximately two pounds. His name was Tom.

It came about this way. Sometimes we caught more trout than we could eat immediately, and we always liked to have a nice trout dinner for new arrivals at Forest Home. So we fixed up a pound, which was nothing more than a good-sized box with holes bored in each end. This we placed at the in-running of a little brook nearby, weighting both the box and the cover with large stones.

One spring we had three lively trout of almost the same size in the pound at one time. Wanting to make an oil painting of a typical Cranberry Lake two-pounder, I decided to use the three as a composite model. After setting up my easel and getting out paints, I would take our largest dishpan down to the pound, fill it with water, put one of the trout in, and bring him back to the cottage to pose. They were all too big for the dishpan, but fortunately their tails were flexible. I soon learned to distinguish them as individuals and gave them the unimaginative names of Tom, Dick, and Harry. Dick and Harry were problem fish. They resented being used as models, splashed water all over the room, and frequently ended on the floor. Tom, on the other hand, was good-natured and docile. He not only was content in the dishpan but would even allow me to turn him partly over on his side, the better to observe his coloring. Dad and I became so fond of him that when the painting was finished he was returned to the depths of Cranberry Lake. Dick and Harry ended their careers in our frying pan.

My first acquaintance with Cranberry Lake in winter came on April 9, 1914. Leaving part of our baggage with Johnny Olson in Wanakena, Dad and I shouldered our packs and walked down the Ranger School road to Pleasant Point at the foot of the Narrows. (We did not trust the ice for the first mile of the river.) There Dad improvised a sled from barrel staves, which held most of our duffel for the remainder of the journey over the ice.

The trip was a memorable one. I had been up and down the Inlet dozens of times before, but always in a boat, with spring, summer, or autumn all around. Now everything was both familiar and strange. We could see *into* the woods on either bank much farther. Boulders, knolls, and ridges invisible even in leafless autumn or early spring were now etched clearly by snow.

When we were well out on Dead Creek Flow, I was suddenly startled by the great body of ice giving a resounding crack, which echoed from shore to shore. Momentarily I thought our added weight had caused it.

A stiff southwest wind at our backs hurried us along down the Flow, past the Peninsula, the little islands, and Joe Indian to the main body of the lake. As we rounded Deremo Point,

Snowshoe Time on Cranberry

Looking east over the Narrows on Inlet Flow, one may trace the route followed by James and Fay Welch from Wanakena to Forest Home over the snow-covered surface of Cranberry Lake. (Photo by Dwight Church)

Daddy, leading, suddenly broke through the ice. The water at this spot was probably ten or fifteen feet deep. But to our great surprise he only went down mid-thigh deep. There was a second layer of ice. Possibly it had remained anchored down to rocks and logs nearby after the lake level had risen and refrozen.

The next morning the mercury stood at four above zero, with three inches of new snow and the sun rising over Curtis Mountain into a clear sky. Never before had I seen anything so white and bright as the surface of the lake. Going out on the ice, I took a picture of our cottage.

Later we walked over to Buck Island and around it, taking pictures of the snow-covered rocks and pines. At Roc's Egg Point I managed to get from the ice to the island and then followed the snow-crusted path to the top of the bluffs for a sweeping view of the lake.

On April 17 we decided to make maple syrup, even though we had none of the facilities usually deemed necessary. We constructed a small arch in front of a boulder from a few bricks and an old stove top with the griddles removed. We had a small sap pan for boiling. We whittled out sap spiles from red-berried elder branches, burning out the pith with a hot wire. With brace and half-inch bit we tapped the large sugar maples nearby, and we found enough pails, cans, and jars to collect the sap that dripped from our elder spiles.

Thereafter we rose at daybreak to drag up dry hardwood saplings for sugar wood and gather the sap before the sun was high enough to weaken the crust. All day we cut wood, stoked the fire, listened to the bubbling in the pan, and enjoyed an occasional whiff of the rising steam and the odors of spring in the woods. Friendly juncos came around for crumbs, and a mourning cloak butterfly fluttered lazily down and lighted on a brown patch of snow-free earth.

The sun set. Twilight deepened in the woods. Back on the ridge a fox yapped. We banked the ruddy arch fire and turned in for a night of dreamless sleep.

We were at the lake about the same time of year in 1916, and my diary contains the following entries for that trip:

"*Friday, March 31:* Dad and I arrived in Wanakena a little after noon. Packed down to the Ranger School, but there was so much slush on the ice that we left our packs there and returned to Wanakena and spent the night with Walter and Mrs. Gates. Wilfred [Morrison] came in this evening for a visit.

"*Saturday, April 1:* Up at 4 A.M. Sherm [Hazelton] was over for breakfast, and afterwards I went to his home to get his sledge to draw our packs on. He and Walter went fishing. Dad and I started down the River at 5 A.M. It had frozen hard last night and the walking was good. Arrived at our cottage about 7:30 A.M. Later I walked over to the Indian Mountain Club to see Will Mott and to telephone. John Howland and family came in today. The slush was ankle deep when I came back. It began raining this afternoon.

"*Monday, April 3:* It froze hard last night so I started for the foot of the lake [Cranberry Lake Village] just before sunrise. Sent mail and brought back an eighteen-pound pack of supplies. We tapped thirty-one sugar maples today. Gathered sap until dark.

"*Tuesday, April 4:* Tapped quite a few more trees.

"*Wednesday, April 5:* Willard [Howland] was over this morning. Gathered sap and kept the arch going this forenoon. We helped Willard, Art [his son], and John Howland bag and load sawdust this afternoon. Then rode down to the foot of the lake, got a packbasket full of food supplies, and walked back with John. Walking none too good. John is going to operate the Indian Mountain Club as a hotel this summer.

"*Thursday, April 6:* We had a snow storm about four o'clock which drove us inside for an hour. The snow came thick and fast with quite a high wind for awhile. And then it passed as suddenly as it had come—perfect quiet, everything covered with nearly an inch of new snow. Nothing showed dark in the woods except the tree trunks and the branches when viewed from beneath. The smaller twigs traced a slender dark line against their snow covering like the delicate veining of leaves. The snow so completely covered the earth with such a pure white that as twilight deepened the light that remained seemed to come as much from beneath as from above.

"*Sunday, April 16:* The sun rose straight over the highest peak of old Curtis this morning. A little later I stepped out of doors. It had frozen hard during the night. The air was very clear and bracing. I could hear faintly the roar of Sucker Brook from beyond Buck Island. The sun had now passed under a thin film of cloud and a half twilight still lingered in the woods. With an ax and a few dry sticks of pine I walked out to the sugar arch and began whittling shavings for a fire.

"It was the birds' hour of song and they were all making the most of it. Near at hand were chickadees and phoebes. Back on the ridge a robin sang. Occasionally a squirrel chattered, and in the distance a woodpecker drummed.

"*Wednesday, April 26:* The warmth and brightness of the sun was welcome after the cold weather. The boat slipped ahead easily and noiselessly under the oar strokes. Rounding the point, my eyes fell upon the personification of the day and season, 'Uncle Steve' Ward, whose two hundred pounds and eighty years rested lightly on his spirit. He was seated comfortably on an upturned box on the dock, fishing.

"Yesterday when I saw him he was pushing and poling two heavily loaded boats through some drift ice which had just closed the channel, causing him an extra hour's labor where he could have rowed through in ten minutes with free water. Yet despite the fact that a rainstorm was rapidly overtaking him, his cheery greeting was as spontaneous as ever.

"*Thursday, May 11:* What a storm! We had to lash the boats down to the dock and could only make each other hear by shouting when out on the point.

"The forest fairly roared, big trees bending like rushes and frequently crashing to the ground, while last year's dry leaves swirled and eddied about. The lake has had some great breakers, but the strangest part was the way in which the wind was constantly whipping and picking up the water until the spray rose as from the foot of a waterfall, often to a height of over fifty feet and an acre in extent. Then, reflecting rainbows, it drove along with incredible swiftness to the farther shore and disappeared. Across the lake the foam occasionally rose higher than the treetops as the waves pounded the shore of Rock Island [one of the Sears Islands]."

Snow was no novelty to us on early spring or late fall trips to Forest Home. One April after the ice had gone out of the lake, there was a sudden snowstorm that left a white blanket several inches thick. My father and I swept several places bare in the back yard, spaded up some earth, and put out crumbs and scraps for the birds. A large number gathered. There were a half-dozen hermit thrushes (the first I ever saw), many juncos, song and white-throated sparrows, and one robin. The next morning I watched chickadees, nuthatches, and a hairy woodpecker. The wood thrush I had been hearing before the snowstorm was silent.

A storm in late March of 1919 lengthened to three days our journey from Lacona to Cranberry, which today takes three hours by car. We spent the first night in Watertown, the second in Wanakena (to which we had had to walk from the railroad station in Benson Mines), and the third at Tramps Retreat. The caretaker had given us the key to the guide house and suggested that we might want to spend the night there.

The following morning it was still snowing. I stepped gingerly out from shore to test the ice. Suddenly, without warning, I dropped through. The water was deep, but by throwing myself quickly sidewise I managed to keep from going in more than waist deep. I did not tarry. Swimming is fine under certain conditions, but not in ice water with a snowstorm raging. Before I could get back to the guide camp, my clothing was stiff with snow and ice. Dad rebuilt the fire to thaw and dry my clothes before we started out again.

Meanwhile, Dad had found two pairs of old snowshoe frames and rigged them with some cord he was carrying. After lunch, with their aid, we managed to get ourselves and our packs safely across the ice to the other side of Dead Creek Flow. The snow was now three feet deep, but it was so light that the snowshoes were more trouble than help in trying to get through the woods. So we hung them up as high as we could in the trees, hoping the porkies would not find them, and started on toward Forest Home. We finally reached the cottage about an hour before dark. As soon as the lake was free of ice about a month later, Dad rowed back to the flow, retrieved the snowshoe frames, and returned them to Tramps Retreat.

Trips to Cranberry in the fall, after the summer people had all left, were also adventurous. An entry in my journal for October 22, 1917, for instance, tells the story of why Haywood Hawk's Island was for many years known as Bear Island.

The day started as a stormy one, with wind and rain. After days of starting out on his trap lines shortly after daylight and returning after dark, my father welcomed the opportunity to stay in camp. But by afternoon the weather cleared, and taking his gun, an old Ithaca 10-gauge with an auxiliary .45-70 rifle barrel on the right side, he rowed across to Joe Indian Island and then turned westward along the shore on the lookout for game.

Much of the surface of the lake was spotted with stumps and tree trunks. Soon he noticed that one of the stumps far ahead seemed to be moving. Looking intently, he decided that it was a bear, swimming away from Joe Indian toward the little islands to the west. Dad remained motionless until the bear reached Haywood Hawk's Island, waded ashore, shook himself, and disappeared into a dense thicket of spruce. Dad rowed to the island, stopped the boat just short of the shore, stepped out into the shallow water, and silently lifted the prow onto a rock. Then he picked up his gun and followed the bear's trail up a narrow path through the spruce toward a campground above a cut bank on the opposite shore. Tiptoeing along, he kept a sharp lookout for the bear and finally caught sight of him, digging into a tin can left by a careless camper. Dad raised his gun and waited for the bear to change position so that he could get a shot at a vital spot.

Suddenly, warned by some wandering air current or his sixth sense, the bear at a single bound went over the brink of the cut bank and disappeared from sight. Dad heard his feet rattle the stones on the beach and the splash as he plunged into the lake. Dad sprinted to the top of the cut bank. Bruin was some distance out, swimming strongly toward Kimball Island. As Dad reached the bank, the bear turned his head to look back, and at that moment a bullet crashed through his skull.

Dad went back for his boat and rowed around the island. After a few precautionary pokes with the oar to make sure his bullet had reached its mark, he tried to lift the bear into the boat. Without the bear's rising noticeably, the boat sank until it took in water. Dad then hitched a bowline around the bear's jaw and towed him back to the shore. He pulled the bear up on the beach, pulled the boat up and turned it on its side, propped it, and then rolled the bear into it. Righting the boat, he launched it and rowed back to Forest Home. Dressed, the bear weighed over two hundred and fifty pounds.

GUIDING, TUTORING, AND NATURE STUDY

My first work as a guide was in May, 1914. Since the Indian Mountain Club was crowded with guests and there were not enough of the old guides to go around, they asked Dad and me to help out. I was assigned to a party going on a two-day trip to Darning Needle Pond. The other guides were George Bancroft and Walter Gates. Overeager, I filled my packbasket with some of the heaviest of the canned goods, and I remember George Bancroft's quiet, kindly words: "You have too heavy a pack there; let me take some of that."

We packed along the trail past Chair Rock Flow, over the lower slopes of Indian Mountain, and across the outlet of Fishpole Pond to the log camp which the club had erected about halfway up the west side of Darning Needle Pond. This camp, like the one at Dog Pond [east of Cranberry Lake], consisted of one large room which served as living room, dining room, and kitchen. Wings on two sides contained four bunks each, with comfortable springs and mattresses. These camps were stocked with blankets and staple foods, so that it was necessary to bring in only our fresh supplies. A rowboat and a canoe were kept in a small boathouse at each camp.

We caught quite a few trout at Darning Needle and some in the nearby ponds. As I think back to my companions on this first trip, I am struck by the fact that guiding was, and is, a fairly hazardous occupation. Within a few years George Bancroft would have his neck dislocated by a storm-thrown tree one wild night as he went down to check his boat in front of the Indian Mountain Club. A few years later Walter Gates would be killed, mistaken for a deer while making a drive.

For some time after this I did more boating than guiding, but then the work stepped up, either because the club was crowded or because certain members specifically requested my services, and for four or five seasons I enjoyed guiding and the many new friends it brought me. What I lacked in experience in fishing around the Cranberry Lake region was partly compensated for by my knowledge of the trees, wild flowers, birds, and animals. These had been my special interest for several years, an interest encouraged by my father, a skillful woodsman and adept trapper; by my mother, who loved the out of doors; and by our family physician, Dr. Newton Cook of Sandy Creek, who had encouraged me to spend months out of my school years in the Adirondacks and had presented me with Chester A. Reed's field guides to birds and wild flowers.

For example, I knew that a certain flower was a red trillium and not a "woods sunflower," a name coined on the spur of the moment by one of the old guides when asked what it was.

I remember other employers who were particularly interested in knowing that a certain bird song from the treetops came from the throat of the rose-breasted grosbeak; that the delicate scent drifting across the lake in late May came from myriads of fire-cherry blossoms on the burned mountain sides; and that a rare patch of trailing arbutus was to be found at a certain spot along the shore of Dog Pond.

Darning Needle Pond, about 1915
Here may be seen the havoc wrought by the forest fires that followed the lumbermen. The far side of the pond was not burned. (Photo by Fay Welch)

A Kingbird's Nest on a Stump in West Flow
The stumps of submerged trees furnished plentiful homes for kingbirds, tree swallows, grackles, and flickers. (Photo by Fay Welch)

At first the old guides were understandably unenthusiastic about a youngster barely out of high school breaking into their group, although no one ever so much as uttered an unkind or disparaging word. Little by little, however, I realized that I was being accepted, in fact welcomed, possibly because I was a willing pack horse, a ready dishwasher, and a fair cook. Within a few years I counted as my very good friends Willard, John, Chan, and Nelt Howland, Wilfred Morrison, George Preston, Sherm Hazelton, Chan Westcott, and of course Walter Gates and George Bancroft. For many years I treasured and used a beautiful paddle, a gift from George Bancroft, who made particularly choice ones by hand. Another which he presented to Dad hangs today, retired from active service, on the wall at our camp.

In addition to the camps at Darning Needle and Dog ponds and Brandy Brook, the club had a somewhat less pretentious one on the shore of Cat Mountain Pond. Some of these camps boasted caretakers who also served as patrolmen. Sherm Hazelton had charge of the Cat Mountain camp one spring when Willard Howland and I packed in with two fishermen. We reached the camp late in the forenoon. After a good substantial noon meal, Willard and Sherm kept the guests entertained for some time with a rare collection of hunting and fishing yarns. Finally Willard, realizing that the inevitable could not be postponed any longer, knocked the ashes out of his pipe and with a sigh turned to Sherm and asked, "Sherm, which one of them old socks do you use for a dishcloth?" I realized that was my cue!

Willard, the eldest of the four Howland brothers, was a wonderful companion; he never hurried, he never got excited, he never worked too hard. He was always quietly glad to see you. His slightly watery blue eyes would twinkle at the slightest provocation, and he was unfailingly optimistic. If the fish were not biting in the ponds, he knew they would be hungry around the spring holes in the lake—"as sure as God made little apples!" He was somewhat above middle height, and spare.

Willard Howland at High Falls (1923)

The eldest of the four Howland brothers, all noted as guides, Willard watches to see if the trout are rising. (Photo by Albert Fowler)

Though well along in years, he changed no more rapidly than some mossy tree trunk.

There was keen competition among the guides at the club, and supposedly some mythical prize was posted for the one whose party landed the largest trout or secured the greatest number in a single day. I didn't consider myself even in the running, but finally one lucky season two men for whom I was guiding landed what later proved to be first place in both categories—and on successive days, too.

Our first day of fishing was a stormy one with a wicked southeast wind blowing. We anchored our motorboat behind the little easterly Roc's Egg Point of Buck Island. In common with other guides I had fished many times on the opposite side of this point, but none of us fished where I was now forced to anchor to be out of the wind. Having towed a skiff behind the motorboat, I took one of the men in the skiff, and we began trolling in the rougher water where we usually fished, leaving the third member of our party to fish from the motorboat. Soon we heard a shout and, looking back, found our friend standing up in the boat with his rod bent almost double. For a fraction of a second I thought he was snagged on bottom until I saw the tip of his rod quiver. Then we made out that his frantic shouts were for the landing net, which we had with us. We swept around and back as fast as possible, shouting encouragement and advice. "Keep him away from the anchor line! Don't let him get around the propeller!" Netted and back at the club, this brook trout neared the four-pound mark.

The next day we decided to try the ponds. Going by motorboat to the head of Dead Creek Flow, we walked up past Glasby to Cat Mountain Pond. Here we split, one man fishing Cat, the other Bassout. In the afternoon they changed places. At the end of the day we had taken fifty trout from Cat Mountain Pond and thirty from Bassout.

Eventually I spent most of my time guiding for Lawrence Griffith, an architect from Yonkers, and his family. Griffith was a delightful companion. We had some wonderful trips together which Larry planned with great relish. I can still see his blue eyes dancing with excitement and his neatly trimmed goatee quivering beneath his ready smile as he smacked his lips over the good meals he had planned for our next three- or four-day trip to Dog Pond. With some help from Mrs. Griffith and their two daughters, Teddy and

Louie, we managed very nicely and had some splendid days and nights together on the trails and around the fireplace in the Dog Pond camp.

After the Indian Mountain Club had dissolved, Larry purchased part of its property, and years later my uncle, Fred Smart, remodeled Larry's cottage and boathouse.

For a few seasons Walter Gates operated a group of cabins and tents around High Falls known as Postern Lodge. On July 18, 1916, I received word from my father, who was there doing carpenter work and guiding, that Walter wished me to come up, as he had guests coming in who needed two guides. Only his hunting and fishing partner, Wilfred Morrison, was available. The country beyond High Falls was completely strange to me, but as I understood that Wilfred was familiar with it I did not hesitate to throw a few personal items in my pack and take off for Postern Lodge.

That night I slept in a tent on a bed of balsam boughs with the pleasant music of the waterfall in my ears, and the next morning we loaded our packs and started up the Oswegatchie with Wilfred in the lead. Wilfred was quite a character. Rumor had it that he was of Scotch-Irish parentage and had been brought up by a French-Canadian family. The result was his indescribable patois-brogue.

Our party consisted of Mr. and Mrs. White, their little dog, Dr. Voorhees (whom Wilfred termed "de lady doctuh"), Miss Voorhees, and Miss Gearhart. The last three were seasoned campers, having tramped and fished around Cranberry for several summers. Each one carried his own personal equipment, while Wilfred's pack and mine were loaded with two days' provisions for seven. Since our plan was to sleep at Fide Scott's old camps on Big Deer Pond the first night and at the Indian Mountain Club on the second night, we did not carry blankets.

We made rather good time along the trail up the Oswegatchie River during the forenoon, passing some huge primeval white pines almost five feet in diameter and reaching

Beaverdam (at this time the only one around Cranberry) about eleven-thirty in the morning. Wilfred and "de lady doctuh" put their fishpoles together and tried their luck from the beaver dam while I started the fire and made preparations for lunch. In a few minutes they were back with enough trout to fill two frying pans. Wilfred and I soon had these done to a turn over the coals, and we all enjoyed a good lunch. After the five-mile pack of the morning and all these trout, no one was in a hurry to start the afternoon trip or thought it necessary, since Big Deer (or Lost Lake, as Verplanck Colvin christened it in 1873) was supposed to be only two miles away.

Dog Pond before Logging Operations
Fay Welch is shown here at the end of the trail from East Flow. The Indian Mountain Club camp was located in the pine grove on the opposite shore. (Photo by James Welch)

High Falls on the Upper Oswegatchie

Postern Lodge was located just to the left, and from here a trail led up the river to the Beaverdam. (Photo by Dwight Church)

After a long siesta we finally got under way, but more than half of the afternoon was gone.

Many years before, Fide Scott supposedly had a trail from his camps to this point, but by now it was practically obliterated, and as Wilfred tried to follow it, it seemed as though every treetop and old log that had fallen during the years had come down across the trail. Some of our party made rather caustic comments about the going, so Wilfred tried to pick out a better way with easier footing. Soon we had lost all trace of the old trail. At one point we crossed a tiny brook, which was welcome as we were thirsty. The day was hot, we were all carrying packs, and the fish had been well salted.

Wilfred led on, zigzagging wherever the going was best, until finally just before sunset a bit of water glistened through the trees far down a slope. Our party rested while Wilfred and one of the girls descended the hill. In a few minutes they were back to report that the water was Big Deer but that we were on the opposite side of the pond from Fide Scott's camps and must circle a fairly extensive swamp. Therefore Wilfred struck back away from the pond, keeping to the high ground.

By this time the sun had set. Wilfred was leading and I was bringing up the rear. I noted rather carefully the direction of the lighter western sky and kept track of this for some time. I had an uneasy feeling that Wilfred never did circle to the right to bring us around toward the camps, but I thought it best to keep quiet. He was already more than a little upset because some of the party had been a bit critical of his pathfinding, and I was afraid any remark of mine questioning his judgment might be just too much. So I assured the others that Wilfred was entirely familiar with the country. To their questions about how soon we would reach the camps, he invariably replied, "I t'ink dey jus' over de nex' ridge."

Night fell, but we stumbled on. Finally we came to a rather level hilltop with huge forest trees ringing a place where Wilfred put down his pack, saying, "I t'ink I look ahead by myself for de camps."

By that time I had no illusions about where we were going to spend the night, so I slipped out of my pack and immediately started gathering firewood. Wilfred came back in a little while without having found any camps. We had a good fire going and were comfortable except for the fact that we were all very thirsty—even the dog, in spite of his having been carried for the last hour. None of us had had a drink of water since midafternoon. Wilfred now went off on a long diagonal some forty-five degrees to one side of our back trail, going as far as he could and still be within sound of our voices. He would halloo from time to time and we would answer him.

While members of our party may have complained a bit in the afternoon, now that they realized we were lost they were the best scouts imaginable. All turned in with a will to help me get firewood and gather boughs, not only for a bed but also to give us some covering, as we had no blankets.

Wilfred returned and set off on a long diagonal to the other side of our back trail. By this time he had dropped all pretense of looking for the camps and was only trying to find water. Once we had water we could settle down for the night fairly comfortably. He returned unsuccessful from this third scouting trip, and now, about eleven o'clock, as there was nothing more to do around the temporary campsite, I set off with him and we went much farther than he had gone on his first trip. Finally we came out of the forest onto a burned hillside with gaunt tree trunks outlined in the starlight above a thicket of raspberry bushes and pin cherry and poplar sprouts. Wilfred, who was down the slope from me, called out that he had found a spring. This was welcome news and I quickly joined him. We both drank deep draughts of the wonderful fresh water and then filled our canteens to take back to the others.

Now for the first time I had a chance to have a good look at the stars and get oriented. Wilfred and I discussed in low tones where we might be. He thought we might be near Mud Lake, but from my very limited knowledge of the country this did not seem likely in view of the direction we had been traveling.

Suddenly I became aware of a very faint, faraway, but familiar sound that I had heard before; yes, only a few hours before. I looked around again, and miraculously the whole scene was suddenly familiar.

"Wilfred!" I exclaimed. "Do you hear that sound?"

He listened and then in amazement said, "Why, dat is de water running over de beaver dam!"

It was. We had practically backtracked, and the spring Wilfred had found was but a few yards from the Oswegatchie River, perhaps a quarter of a mile above the point where we had left it.

We were both greatly relieved to discover where we were.

But then Wilfred had a second, sobering thought. "Fay, if we go back and tell dem where we are, dey will want to walk all de way back to High Falls tonight!" As such a trip would have taken most of the remainder of the night and brought disgrace upon both Wilfred and me as guides, we finally decided we would tell them that we now knew where we were but would keep quiet about the exact place.

So we returned with the water, which was most welcome, and then spent a not-too-uncomfortable night, catnapping with our feet to the fire. Soon after daylight, having eaten a bit of dry food, we started once more for Big Deer and before long arrived at the old Fide Scott cabins. I must admit some of the country we passed over looked vaguely familiar.

Fide Scott had been dead for several years, but two of his camps remained. One was a sleeping cabin with a fireplace whose chimney was made of long poles, the butts set around three sides of a rectangle some three by five feet with tops drawn much closer at the upper part of the chimney. Within this wooden framework flat stones, chinked with mud, had been built up to a height of three or four feet. This served as a fireplace as long as it was used with great discretion. If anyone had ever piled on too much wood, the whole place would have quickly gone up in smoke, the fireplace and the chimney going first.

While our guests rested in this cabin, Wilfred and I prepared a more substantial brunch over a half-fallen-apart cookstove in the adjoining building. Wilfred was feeling very low; he said nothing for a long time and then finally, between the flipping of flapjacks, moaned, "I am so tam discourage I could cut my own t'roat!"

Because Wilfred felt so badly about getting lost more or less in his own back yard, we all agreed to say nothing about our adventure outside of our own group.

We loafed for the remainder of the day at the camp. That evening we went down to the shore of the pond and watched seventeen deer feeding in its shallows. The next day we followed the trail by Tamarack and Slender ponds to Cowhorn and along Six Mile Creek past Sliding Falls to the Indian Mountain Club. There our guests and Wilfred spent the night, while I returned to Forest Home, a mile away.

Little was said about our trip for two years, although I did have to turn aside a few questions from Dad about why we had taken three days for the trip instead of the two we had planned. Then one evening at Wanakena I met Walter Gates, who was on his way to the Indian Mountain Club. I had a motorboat and invited him to ride down to camp with me. On the way we were caught in a bad thunderstorm, and after waiting it out on one of the islands we reached Forest Home after dark. Dad had a good fire going, and we talked Walter into drying out and spending the night with us before we took him to the Indian Mountain Club the following morning.

As we were getting ready for bed, I heard Walter and Dad chuckling over some joke. Finally Walter called out, "Fay, how did you like your bed that first night over by Big Deer?"

Then it came out. A few days before, he had been guiding one of the Doctor's friends, and the story had been too good to keep any longer.

A few weeks later there was a big group at the Indian Mountain Club, and all of the local guides were rounded up to help out. Wilfred and Walter were there, plus the Howlands, Dad, and a number of others. After supper, as was our custom, we all sat around on the back porch talking over hunting and fishing trips. During a lull in the conversation Walter gave me a slight wink and turning to Wilfred, said, "Wilfred, when we're through here let's go back to your Camp Betsy." This was on the Inlet near Five Ponds. "And," Walter continued, "what do you say we go by Six Mile Creek and over by Big Deer to Beaverdam? You know the country up that way pretty well, don'tcha?"

Without indicating in any way that he had heard Walter, Wilfred remarked in a flat voice, "I hab me a boat up on de river; I mus' feex him."

The most beautiful Cranberry Lake island, in fact one of the loveliest in the entire Adirondacks, is Buck Island, second largest in the modern lake. Before the building of the dam in 1867, it had been the largest, but the dam raised the water some thirteen or fourteen feet and formed Joe Indian Island from what had once been a large peninsula. Buck Island, some twenty-one acres in extent, is almost a perfect circle except for two deep and narrow bays, indistinguishable a half mile away, which nearly cut off the small section on which the late Judge Irving G. Vann built his summer home many years ago. There is also the tiny point on the east side called Roc's Egg Point. The highest spot near the center of the island is about 115 feet above lake level.

The rocky shore of the island rises abruptly, almost precipitously, from the water in all but a few sandy spots. On rocks near the water line a constant struggle goes on between the lichens and the waves. Farther up the rocks the elephant's ears, reindeer lichens, and mosses gain a permanent foothold, and eventually wintergreen and heath shrubs are succeeded by pine, spruce, and paper birch. On the east side the Four Sentinels, a group of huge red pines two or three times the height of the other trees, stood guard for many years.

Here on Buck Island during the summers of 1917 and 1918 it was my good fortune to be part guide, part tutor, and part companion to the four grandchildren of Judge Vann—Katherine, fifteen; Albert, thirteen; and the twins, Ruth and Betty, ten. Their father, Albert P. Fowler, had passed away not long before, and Mrs. Fowler arranged for me to be with the children for a large part of each day during July and August.

On rainy days we read aloud from Scott, Thoreau, and Ray Stannard Baker, better known under the pen name David Grayson. And we played checkers and tutored a bit in history and English.

But when the weather was fine we ranged over the island or along nearby mainland trails, or even to more distant places—Sliding Falls, the top of Indian Mountain, Olmstead and Dog

Ponds—fishing, exploring, camping. We made rock collections and cataloged the trees, shrubs, wild flowers, lichens, and fungi on the island. We discovered that a cross section of the larger tree trunks, especially the poplars, was a reliable compass, for the prevailing winds had caused these trees to have an east-west diameter three or four inches greater than their north-south axis. Temporarily we added to the species of ferns on the island when Kay and I made a rustic stretcher to carry clumps of maidenhair and royal fern down the Sucker Brook trail, transported them to the island, and set them out on Roc's Egg Point. We cooked amazingly good outdoor meals over open fires on two neighboring islands that the Judge had named "Katherine" and "Albert" for his grandchildren. I can still taste the brook trout broiled over the coals, the potatoes roasted in the ashes, the steaming hot cocoa, the bacon and eggs.

Dry and brittle lichens still clung to the stones of the fireplaces in the main camp. We read that a fungous outer layer of the lichen permits the delicate drought-sensitive algae within to exist for a long time without the water usually essential to life. So Albert and I started pouring a little water on the lichens of the dining-room fireplace each day after lunch. At first the water did no more than roll off from the dusty surface, but we persevered and eventually were astonished and rewarded by finding that the lichen was still alive. It became soft and flexible and somewhat greener in color. I believe these rocks had been in the fireplace twenty years at that time.

It is said that the island was burned over about 1845. In 1961 a few charred stumps were still visible.

In 1920 I wrote in a survey that appeared in the *Empire Forester* the following year:

"In considering the trees upon the island three forest types are recognized. In type 1 yellow birch is dominant. Type 2 is not as truly a forest type in the sense that the white birch will eventually occupy the soil even though at present it comprises three-fourths of the stands. [Much of the white birch remains today.] The conifers dominate type 3.

A Loon's Nest

Always built near the water, the loon's nest is about three feet in diameter. This nest was located on one of the floating bogs near West Flow. (Photo by Fay Welch)

"The largest hardwoods upon the island are found in type 1. Here is one yellow birch measuring 42 inches in diameter and estimated to be about 435 years old. A 17-inch birch, an 18-inch sugar maple, and 27 and 30-inch hemlock are also found. In 1914 there were five Norway (red) pines on the east side of the island, of which but one is left which measures 24 inches and reaches a height twice that of the surrounding trees. A nearby stump 30 inches in diameter is over 200 years old. These trees and some 24-inch white pine undoubtedly played an important role in the reseeding of the island after the fire. The cherries and shadbush (*Amelanchier*) were probably started by seeds deposited by birds, while the poplars were wind sown."

In addition to the trees already mentioned, the following woody plants were noted in 1920: red, mountain, and striped maples, mountain ash, white cedar (arborvitae), balsam, willow, alder, red-berried elder, witch hopple, twin and bush honeysuckles, ground hemlock (or American yew), blueberries, skunk currant, spiraea, three or four clumps of juniper, and a small patch of trailing arbutus.

"One of the most interesting associations upon the island," I wrote, "is found near the eastern end of the bluffs. Here the rocks rise at an angle of forty degrees for nearly one hundred feet, and beginning just above high water mark and extending nearly to the top is typical bog vegetation. There are mats of sphagnum moss over a foot in depth, which support Labrador tea, sheep laurel, sweet gale, and leatherleaf."

This bog vegetation on Buck Island recalls the fact that Cranberry Lake was once perhaps unique among Adirondack lakes in having many floating bogs. Today few of these are left, but early in the century there were a number of them.

These were extensive mats of vegetation, the roots and the earth they were mixed with forming a platform two to four feet in depth and supporting a dense growth of bog plants, particularly shrubs such as leatherleaf, Labrador tea, sweet gale, sheep laurel, blueberries, chokeberries, and occasionally cranberries. Often there was considerable sphagnum moss around the roots of these shrubs. It was best to wear boots when exploring the bogs, as they would often sink under your feet until the water covered your ankles. Unless you exercised care you might step into a hole that went directly into the lake.

The largest of these, the Big Bog, was located near the fringes of the Hopyard, westerly from Joe Indian Island. It was perhaps two acres in extent and had a few small tamarack trees growing on it. This bog was unique in that it had a little lagoon about twenty-five feet in diameter near its center. The bogs were a haven for wildlife, especially otter and mink. Many of the loons that inhabited the lake built their nests at the border of the bogs, and later beaver constructed their houses upon them. I caught my first mink on a bog in West Flow, and Dad shot an otter in the lagoon of the Big Bog.

Originally these bogs were probably swampy areas adjacent to the old lake. When the new lake flowed over them, the dense mass of roots proved buoyant enough to raise entire sections of bog some fourteen feet to the surface. Most of them were anchored in place for many years by tree trunks which remained rooted to the bottom but projected upward through the bog. During recent decades, however, most of these anchors have rotted away, and ice and wave action have combined to break up and dislodge the bogs until now it is hard to find traces of many of them. When on October 14, 1961, I set out to visit the Big Bog, I found only a remnant of it left, perhaps one-tenth its former area, and from this three separate sections had been shredded and were lodged nearby. A beaver house with fresh cuttings was located on the back side, and there were signs of mink all around the shore. In a few years the Big Bog will probably follow its former companions from West Flow, Joe Indian Island, Dead Creek Flow, and the Peninsula into oblivion.

FORESTRY CAMP AND RANGER SCHOOL COME TO CRANBERRY

All of us around Cranberry Lake were excited in the spring of 1915 by the report that students from the New York State College of Forestry at Syracuse University were going to set up a camp beside the mouth of Sucker Brook.

Soon faculty and students appeared and started clearing the camp site of the brush that had grown up since the area was abandoned about ten years before by the McDonald pulping interests. Two small secondhand motorboats and a small flat-bottomed scow brought in most of the equipment and many students. With lumber from abandoned logging camps, a thirty-six by sixteen foot storehouse was built at a total cost of $60.85, and a tennis court was constructed on a site where a chum and I had made a feeble beginning a year or so before. Students and faculty were housed in tents, and a larger tent served as dining hall and classroom. Between the faculty tents a little gully ran down to a beautiful sand beach and excellent swimming. Sucker Brook Flow on the south side of the camp provided a perfect landlocked harbor.

At first the Sucker Brook site on Barber's Point, was used by permission of the J. J. Barber Estate. In 1923

FAY WELCH

Charles Lathrop Pack purchased the property and deeded it to Syracuse University for the use of the College of Forestry.

As a neighbor I remember the first camps chiefly for their water meets and exciting canoe and swimming races and for the wonderful sings around a big roaring campfire, in which many of the neighboring cottagers joined.

During the summer of 1918 I hauled all students, faculty, guests, and supplies to and from the camp in a seven-passenger inboard motorboat belonging to my uncle, Fred Smart. When a quantity of baggage or an extra number of students needed transportation, we towed a scow or a string of canoes.

The Forestry Summer Camp

Sucker Brook Flow and Gertrude Island (*center*) with the Forestry Summer Camp on Barber Point on the right. Katherine Island is at upper left. The College of Forestry at Syracuse University opened the Forestry Camp in 1915, continuing summer training of students through 1966. This picture was taken following reconstruction after World War II. (Photo by Dwight Church)

As the summers passed, I was impressed by the tremendous amount of work accomplished by the students in their one-hour work periods each morning and on Saturday forenoons. Huge log retaining walls along the crumbling sandbanks were built, and docks, boathouses, a kitchen, and many other buildings were added by successive classes. Later on, as a student and then as a member of the staff, I found that this camp experience was a priceless opportunity really to get to know one's classmates as well as the forest and to have close personal contact with many of the department heads, whom we seldom met at college. Here we had an opportunity for practical field work in many subjects which had seemed rather academic in Syracuse: dendrology, ecology, sylviculture, entomology, pathology, mensuration, surveying, and forest protection. Living in tents, sharing in the hardships and the building of the camp, and working together in the woods with the black flies, punkies, mosquitoes, and forest fires tended to separate the men from the boys. Each one gained a better idea of what the life of a forester was like, and all gained in self-confidence and resourcefulness. Years later a survey of the alumni of the college showed that the part of their four years of training best remembered and deemed most valuable by a majority of the graduates was the time spent at Summer Camp.

During most of the early years the camp was of twelve weeks' duration, but in 1929 it was shortened to ten. Students were expected to attend the camp following completion of their sophomore year. Attendance varied from fifteen in 1918 to sixty in 1922. When World War II cut enrollment to eight students in 1943, the camp was closed and instruction was given at the Ranger School. This arrangement was continued in 1944 and 1945.

After World War II a construction program was undertaken which ultimately resulted in cabins for all the students, classroom buildings, and the installation of flush toilets, hot and cold water, fluorescent lighting, and other conveniences. The camp began to resemble a summer school. It became a

The Ranger School

Founded in 1912 by the College of Forestry on a tract of land given by the Rich Lumber Company, the school is still in use by the College for the year-round training of forest rangers. (Photo by Dwight Church)

more efficient place to work, but some of the characteristics which had caused earlier students to value the summer experience so highly were lost.

For many years practically all of the students of the college attended Summer Camp. Beginning in 1955, however, one major group after another started substituting other experiences until only students electing the general forestry curriculum went to the camp, and this after their freshman year.

For most students and Cranberry Lake residents, Summer Camp is inextricably linked with the name of Professor C. C. Delavan. Del, as he was called, successfully directed the camp for twenty-seven years. From 1957 through 1964 Professor John W. Barrett was director, and in 1965 Professor Harry Burry. The camp was not open in 1966. The buildings at Sucker Brook remained empty and abandoned except for a caretaker. In the summer of 1967 the camp for forestry students was transferred to the Pack Demonstration Forest near Warrensburg, and the camp on Cranberry Lake was reopened as the "Cranberry Lake Field Biology Station," jointly operated by the College of Forestry and the State University Center at Albany.

Summer Camp was not the only branch of the State College of Forestry at Cranberry Lake, nor was it the first. The New York State Ranger School mentioned above was established in 1912 on a tract of 1,814 acres, a gift of the Rich Lumber Company. The dean of the college, Hugh P. Baker, selected the site for the school buildings on the northwest side of the Inlet Flow just below the Narrows and about a mile and a quarter from Wanakena. This is only a few hundred yards from the boundary of a magnificent stand of primeval forest, part of the New York State Forest Preserve. Thus students have an opportunity to study a rare primitive area, in sharp contrast to the cut and burned-over lands of the Summer Camp forest. The object of the Ranger School is, in the words of one of its directors, James F. Dubuar, "to train men to fill the gap between the average woodsman and the professional forester."

The first director of the school was Philip Tripp Coolidge, who was assisted successively by Russell T. Gheen and Reuben P. Prichard. Most of the school work was carried on out of doors. On very stormy days classes were held indoors, at first in the students' living quarters in Wanakena. Students and faculty, with a few helpers, erected buildings on the site below the Narrows, put up a telephone line, cleared land, dug stumps, and dragged sunken logs from the lake to clear a passage to the main channel.

In November, 1912, everyone moved into the first building, a shedlike affair with no plumbing that served as kitchen, dining room, bunkhouse, and classroom—and in later years as a woodshed and shop. The students cut their own fuel wood and ice.

Five wall tents with wooden platforms were erected to meet the increased enrollment after World War I, and these proved more popular with the students than the dormitory rooms, even in winter. Eventually, more comfortable quarters were provided for both students and faculty. Many buildings have been added in late years to care for the growing student body, which reached ninety in 1966. Gifts of additional acreage have rounded out the property of the school to its present 2,330 acres.

James F. Dubuar guided the Ranger School as director for thirty-seven years, beginning in 1921. He was succeeded in 1957 by Lucian P. Plumley, a graduate of the school and of the College of Forestry, who has held the position till the time of this writing. As this chapter is in final editing, Mr. Plumley's retirement in June, 1967, has been announced.

By the 1966 year end 1,768 men had completed the Ranger School course. Almost one-third of these continued their formal education in college, largely at the College of Forestry at Syracuse. Many alumni have had distinguished careers. Two are vice-presidents of large paper companies; one is a retired vice-admiral; one became director of natural resources of a Canadian province; another became assistant commissioner for lands and forests in the New York State Conservation Department.

A Long Sunday in May*

It was nearly eight o'clock on a rainy Saturday evening when, walking across the Forestry Camp quadrangle, I suddenly noticed two or three bright rifts in the clouds over the west shore hills. I soon had the motorboat under way and in a short time was at the Indian Mountain House waiting to get a call through to the Inlet telling my friends that if the morning were pleasant I would be there at seven, ready to make our contemplated trip.

I awakened Sunday morning a little before five when I heard my father stirring about downstairs preparing breakfast.

Buck Island, a third of a mile away, was entirely obscured by the morning mist when the motorboat swung around the point away from Forest Home. However, some portion of the shore line was visible all the time during the first ten minutes, and at Haywood Hawk's Island I suddenly ran out of the fog. There was a heavy bank across the flow just beyond the islands. It was a pale purple below and was tinted pink above by the first rays of the sun, as yet invisible. Before the boat reached this second bank the sun showed as a clear, blood-red disk through the top of the main fog bank above the lake. It soon paled as I entered the second bank until it resembled the moon in color. Gradually all traces of the shore line were lost. Two islands loomed up to the right and, as I passed, disappeared. Only the floating logs and snags were visible. I steered for a while by the sun until that too disappeared. There was not a breath of air to aid in keeping the direction, but there was noth-

*Editor's note: In the first few decades of the century trails and lumber roads through the Cranberry woods made day-long tramps easy and tempting. Perhaps the route chosen was the swing by Fishpole Pond to Grass Pond or Mud Lake and back by way of Darning Needle Pond after stops at Scott and John ponds; or up Six Mile Creek past Sliding Falls to Cowhorn, Grassy, Slender, and Big Deer ponds, down Fide Scott's old route to High Falls, and back to the lake at Janack's Landing at the head of Dead Creek Flow. Even more tempting, perhaps, was the twenty-five miles of canoeable waters up the winding Oswegatchie above Inlet, combined with side trips afoot. In the entry in his journal for Sunday, May 26, 1918, Fay Welch recorded such a journey.

The Making of a Woodsman

ing to obliterate the wake which the boat left. I tried to keep a straight course by sighting back along this, although it was impossible to see for more than fifty yards in any direction.

F AY W ELCH

I was rather worried about what luck I would have in judging the correct time to make the turn to the right in order to strike the channel around Hawk's Nest. But suddenly there began to be a hint of blue sky above, and a hundred yards farther on the boat shot out of the mist entirely.

I was shivering by the time I reached Wanakena. After tying the boat at the picnic ground, I crossed the bridge and struck into the trail leading up the river. A herring gull standing on a big rock midway in the river allowed me to come close but flew as I reached for the camera.

The previous rain and a heavy dew had saturated the undergrowth so that I soon decided a drenching could not be avoided. Forgetting about the wetting, I enjoyed to the full the fresh morning. Bird songs filled the woods. A mist still hung above the river as it rushed down over the rocks. The moisture on the shadbush and mountain holly gave their leaves a frosted look, while it slid clear or hung in big drops on the thick, waxy leaves of the withe rod. The new half-open fronds of the cinnamon and interrupted ferns growing along the bank appeared molded from crisp seafoam lightly tinted green. The most frequent flower was the Clintonia. The Solomon's-seal and wild sarsaparilla were newly blossomed, and the bunchberry flowers were just attaining a pure white. A few flowers were left on the fire cherries, but the mountain hollies were already forming noticeable green fruits.

At the rapids three boys from the Ranger School who had camped there in a tent were washing and preparing breakfast. I stopped to shout a few words of greeting above the roar of the water and then hurried on.

I was brought up suddenly by the rare beauty of a clump of pink lady-slipper orchids almost in the trail, the first I had seen this year. Finally, still water, an opening in the woods, a whitethroat, and a bend in the river heralded the end of this preliminary journey of seven miles by water and three by trail. Crossing a brook and a little grass plot flecked with blue violets, I reached the footbridge across the river at ten after seven, forty-five minutes after leaving the boat.

At the camp in the clearing [Inlet] the last hurried preparations for our trip were made. Hunting trousers, moccasins, and a pair of heavy woolen socks made me dry and comfortable. We carried a light canoe down to the river and loaded in the lunch, fishing tackle, collecting can, and camera. Then Mary Outterson, the guide George Pinner, and I, one at a time, carefully took our places. Shoving away from the bank and waving goodbye to Mrs. Cadwell, we dipped our paddles in the first strokes of what was to be a thirty-mile canoe trip.

Our objective was Five Ponds, or rather one of them. We were resolved, however, not to be rushed but to journey upstream until weariness or the lateness of the hour forced us to turn about and drift back.

From a point a few hundred yards above the camp to Otter Creek, the country on either side of the river had been burned and lumbered and now was covered with second growth. Above the Beaver Meadows, however, we were never out of sight of virgin forest lying to the west and south. Farther on, the river flowed through it.

Alders overhung the water, and between their roots were big clumps of meadow rue. Sometimes fresh grasses, sedges, and dried meadowsweet replaced the alders. The twin honeysuckle and Cassandra were nearly through blossoming. We paused to have a look at the clump of mountain honeysuckle that I had discovered a week earlier. It was still in bloom. Most beautiful of all among the riverbank dwellers were the graceful, pendulous racemes of chokecherry blossoms.

Twice, brilliant red-winged blackbirds fluttered from top to top of the alders beside us, "chucking" or voicing a plaintive "please," as we passed near their nests. Two black ducks, probably the same pair we had seen the previous Saturday, circled above us several times. A rose-breasted grosbeak, the first Mary had ever seen, perched singing in a dead tree about fifty feet away.

At first the canoe leaked quite a bit, but after we had pulled it up and emptied out the water a couple of times we had no more trouble. The river was very crooked. It was a rare thing to be able to see ahead for a hundred yards. At one place in its wanderings it washed the foot of a ledge, known as High Rock, jutting out from the hills to the east. Here we landed at a little natural granite wharf and scrambled to the top for a view of the country.

At our feet and stretching away at either side was the flat through which the river twisted and swept in half-visible curves. To the north a canoe came into view at a bend in the river and disappeared behind the alders. A moment later a second followed. Across from the river bottom were long hills covered with virgin timber. On the brow of one of the hills far to the left, the tops of a fine group of pines stood out against the skyline, and George said that just beyond them lay the ponds.

Going back to the boat, we found some exceptionally luxuriant clusters of wintergreen berries. We twisted along up the river, digging hard as the strong current caught us at the sharp turns. The other canoes, less heavily loaded and smaller, passed us. We soon reached virgin forest and the loveliest stretch of the river. On the right the bank rose abruptly to a height of several feet and was covered with good-sized conifers—balsam, hemlock, spruce, and a few pines. On the left were the alders, cherries, blue-green tamaracks, and a few darker balsams, with the river disappearing around a bend a little way ahead.

Time had passed so rapidly that we doubted somewhat our ability to reach our first goal. But we lengthened our strokes and dug harder, passing the next mile or two rather quickly. The sun was high by this time. We had paddled nearly four hours. Finally, as we passed underneath a leaning birch, George told us that at the next turn we could see Wilfred Morrison's camp. Sure enough, at the end of a straight stretch and located on the outside of the bend so as to command a view both up and down the river was Camp Royal, later called Camp Betsy. Our friends, who had passed us, were having their lunch here.

We landed, pulled up the canoe, gathered up our duffel, and took the trail up the hill. It was a steep climb at the beginning, and I let my feet run away with my judgment to such an extent that we were forced to stop to catch our breath before reaching the top. Here the trail ran along a very narrow ridge, then down and across a rather wet flat where there were clumps of blue iris and very large blue violets, then across a good-sized brook, and finally into green timber.

The trail twisted up a narrow valley. On the left a mountain brook gurgled down over mossy stones, a delight to the eye as it caught the flickering sunlight. Farther on, it flowed quietly among alder beds. To the right rose a steep hillside. Tall spruce, hemlock, and birch towered above a nearly clean forest floor carpeted with wood sorrel mixed with Clintonia, club mosses, and occasional witch hopple. In these cool woods the fawn lilies and spring beauties were still blossoming.

Two or three times we rested for a few moments, but the mosquitoes dissuaded us from tarrying long. At one of these stops, after we had been walking for an hour, George left us comfortably seated upon a big birch beside the trail while he scouted ahead to see if we were nearing Big Shallow Pond. He was scarcely out of sight when we heard a loud splash in the creek and then a shout. Coming up, we found that he had started a deer out of the water just at the outlet of the pond.

The little pond had a lovely setting. The surrounding woods were chiefly evergreens. Among them the fresh light green of a few hardwoods stood out crisply. A high steep hill topped with pines rose abruptly from the western shore, and at the southern end were many small blue-green tamaracks. Around the shore was a low circle of heath shrubs, the lilac-pink blossoms of the rare swamp laurel showing here and there. The white flower heads of the Labrador tea were just opening, and scattered over the surface of the pond were a few yellow lilies.

By the landing was a stand of pure spruce. Here we kindled a fire and ate our lunch—all of it. I for one was hungry, after eight hours and a twenty-five-mile journey between breakfast and lunch. Before finishing, I heard a splash and looked around in time to see George, who had been launching the boats kept there, scramble dripping out of the pond. We laughed unsympathetically. As we could see and as George had proved, the boats were very small and tricky. Our choice was a light canoe, one end of which had been broken off by a plunge over High Falls and patched two years before by my father. The other was a guide-boat about half the size of the canoe.

We cut some spruce boughs for seats and, using proper care, we found the canoe to be very serviceable, but George had trouble with the guide-boat. To begin with, he gave us the only paddle, while he procured a pole some two or three inches in diameter and about ten feet in length. He held this in both hands crosswise of the boat. Sitting flat on the bottom and rotating the ends in small circles so that they dipped alternately, he splashed about the pond. But soon there was, as George declared, more water within than without. The boat did not merely leak; the water formed a miniature fountain as it came in through one of the holes. George tried sitting in one end so as to raise the hole out of water, but that only resulted in all the water running down underneath and around him. Finally he pulled the boat out, spent some time trying to fix it, and then poled out again.

Big Shallow was an appropriate name for the pond. At no place did I find the water more than three feet deep. The bottom was rather muddy and covered in spots with vegetation. We floated and paddled about, Mary casting as far away from the canoe as possible. She caught two trout and had several more strikes. We could usually see the fish through the clear water. They were small, averaging seven to eight inches.

Clouds now covered the sky and once a few drops of rain

fell. I paddled near the shore and cut a few laurel branches with their exquisite flower clusters. Mary rightly surmised that I was more interested in the flowers than in the fish.

The people whom we had left at the camp now arrived. George very kindly let them take his boat. One of them paddled out hilariously, but soon came hurrying back to shore while George shouted encouragement. It was now three o'clock and our time was limited, so we paddled ashore and were soon tramping back down the trail. Before entering the cut-over land, we paused a few moments where the trail led away from the creek, and in silence tried to fix in our memories the picture made by the brook and the forest. Farther on we stopped again for a drink as we crossed Wolf Creek. Mary gathered some exceptionally large blue violets and placed them in the collecting can.

Returning downstream, I took the stern paddle so that George could fish. The current now carried us along as rapidly as we had been able to go when working hard on the way up. It was my first experience at river canoeing. The current soon taught me several of its tricks. Two or three times after rounding a sharp turn we were swept broadside against the alders, but thanks to my seasoned crew no accident resulted.

As we neared the good fishing holes, I would catch hold of the alders, and with a tug and swerve the canoe would settle back against the current while Mary and George cast ahead or across into some deep eddy or below some big rock or log. At one of the first of these Mary pulled in a twelve-inch trout. At most of them she got her hook snagged, which evoked rather caustic comments from George. Then at his "No fish here," we would swing out and on.

The trip was altogether pleasanter than the one of the morning. The glaring sunlight of the forenoon was gone and the soft cloud light added greatly to the charm of the foliage colors. These rare and delicate colors would not again be equaled until autumn magic touched the forest. The fragrance of the chokecherries drifted on the still air in soft, narrow bands across the river from each bush. We steadied the canoe under an overhanging bush on the left-hand bank while George and I cut several branches. Brought within arm's length, however, they lost much of their charm; the odor especially was too cloying.

I heard a peculiar, half-familiar sound far off, a sort of hollow, not unmusical "tumping." "Did you hear that bittern?" asked George. This was my first formal introduction to the boom of the bittern.

Hearing the voice of Mr. Moore and a companion behind us, we speeded up and for a while had great sport dashing along the straight stretches and switching around the sharp turns. George would catch and drag a bit at the alders on the inner side of the sharpest curves so that we could make the turn without slackening our pace. We held our own against the other canoes until we reached the spot where George had forgotten his hat on the way up. There they passed us.

We might have seen deer in the Beaver Meadows if we had kept silent, but that was impossible. From Otter Creek down seemed but a short distance. The wood thrush was just beginning its vesper song as we rounded the balsam point above the Cadwell camp about six-thirty, and farther back we could hear a rose-breasted grosbeak.

Mrs. Cadwell had a good supper waiting for us, which we thoroughly enjoyed. I still had a ten-mile trip to make before reaching home. Bidding them all goodbye, I set off down the trail. I gathered a few flowers and fungi along the way.

It was twilight when I started the boat back down the river. The engine chugged along faithfully. I piled the cushions in the stern. I was comfortably tired all over, with mind and body relaxed after a day of vigorous exercise and complete enjoyment. Coming down the flow, I nearly fell asleep.

It was practically dark when I finally reached Forest Home. I was soon in bed and thinking drowsily of the trip: fourteen miles by motorboat, thirty by canoe, and nine afoot—fifty-three miles in all, a goodly Sabbath day's journey.

Skyview of Cranberry Lake

Looking northeast from Dead Creek Flow, Bear Mountain is shown at the top, center, with Brandy Brook Flow to the right, and Joe Indian Island, the largest in the lake, just below. Cranberry Lake Village lies to the extreme left, just out of the picture. (Photo by Dwight Church)

These are some of my recollections of early years at Cranberry Lake. Today, of all the vast primeval forest that encircled the lake in 1903, only one small tract remains and that because in the previous century it had become a part of the New York State Forest Preserve, to be forever kept, according to the State Constitution, as wild forest lands. This tract lies on either side of the Inlet, starting below the Ranger School, surrounding the Hawk's Nest, and extending south to Lansing's Point on Dead Creek Flow. To find a large tract of virgin timber in the Cranberry region today, one must go south of Five Ponds or High Falls.

FAY WELCH

In the vicinity of the lake, much of the land that was lumbered and burned was later sold to the state, and it too became part of the Forest Preserve—too late to save its incomparable forests, its valuable topsoil, and much of its water-holding capacity, but in time to assure that it will not be further despoiled or built up and will be kept for the use of the public in camping, hunting, fishing, and exploring.

Now the primeval forest is gone from the slopes around the lake, the trout are gone from the lake, and the beauty of Curtis, Dog, Darning Needle, and other ponds has been so marred that several generations will be needed to restore it. But much that is thrilling remains: the contours of the mountains, the wild calls of the loons, the music of the streams, the sweep of the storms, and the sequence of the seasons. Cranberry Lake, to all who know it, is still a name with magic in it.

Index OF PERSONS AND PLACES